A2
KEY 1

WITH ANSWERS

AUTHENTIC PRACTICE TESTS

Cambridge University Press
www.cambridge.org/elt

Cambridge Assessment English
www.cambridgeenglish.org

Information on this title: www.cambridge.org/9781108694636

First published 2019
20 19 18 17 16 15 14 13 12 11 10 9 8 7 6 5 4 3

Printed in Italy by Rotolito S.p.A.

A catalogue record for this publication is available from the British Library

ISBN 978-1-108-69463-6 Key 1 Student's Book with answers with Audio
ISBN 978-1-108-71812-7 Key 1 Student's Book without answers
ISBN 978-1-108-71813-4 Audio CDs (2)

The publishers have no responsibility for the persistence or accuracy of URLs
for external or third-party internet websites referred to in this publication, and
do not guarantee that any content on such websites is, or will remain, accurate
or appropriate. Information regarding prices, travel timetables, and other factual
information given in this work is correct at the time of first printing but the
publishers do not guarantee the accuracy of such information thereafter.

Contents

Introduction

This collection of four complete practice tests contains papers from the *Cambridge English Qualifications A2 Key* examination. Students can practise these tests on their own or with the help of a teacher.

The *A2 Key* examination is part of a series of Cambridge English Qualifications for general and higher education. This series consists of five qualifications that have similar characteristics but are designed for different levels of English language ability. The *A2 Key* certificate is recognised around the world as a basic qualification in English.

Cambridge English Qualifications	CEFR Level	UK National Qualifications Framework Level
C2 Proficiency	C2	3
C1 Advanced	C1	2
B2 First	B2	1
B1 Preliminary	B1	Entry 3
A2 Key	A2	Entry 2

Further information

The information contained in this practice book is designed to be an overview of the exam. For a full description of all of the above exams, including information about task types, testing focus and preparation, please see the relevant handbooks which can be obtained from the Cambridge Assessment English website at: **cambridgeenglish.org**.

The structure of *A2 Key*: an overview

The *Cambridge English Qualifications A2 Key* examination consists of three papers:

Reading and Writing: 60 minutes
Candidates need to be able to understand simple written information such as signs and newspapers, and produce simple written English.

Listening: 30 minutes approximately
Candidates need to show they can follow and understand a range of spoken materials such as announcements, when people speak reasonably slowly.

Speaking: 8–10 minutes
Candidates take the Speaking test with another candidate or in a group of three. They are tested on their ability to take part in different types of interaction: with the examiner, with the other candidate and by themselves.

	Overall length	Number of tasks/ parts	Number of items
Reading and Writing	60 mins	7	32
Listening	approx. 30 mins	5	25
Speaking	8–10 mins	2	–
Total	approx. 1 hour 40 mins		

Grading

All candidates receive a Statement of Results and candidates whose performance ranges between CEFR Levels A1 and B1 (Cambridge English Scale scores of 100–150) also receive a certificate.

- Candidates who achieve **Grade A** (Cambridge English Scale scores of 140–150) receive the Key English Test certificate stating that they demonstrated ability at Level B1.

- Candidates who achieve **Grade B** or **C** (Cambridge English Scale scores of 120–139) receive the Key English Test certificate at Level A2.

- Candidates whose performance is below A2 level, but falls within **Level A1** (Cambridge English Scale scores of 100–119), receive a Cambridge English certificate stating that they have demonstrated ability at Level A1.

For further information on grading and results, go to the website (see page 5 for details).

Speaking: an overview for candidates

The Speaking test lasts 8–10 minutes. You will take the test with another candidate. There are two examiners but only one of them will talk to you. The examiner will ask you questions and ask you to talk to the other candidate.

Part 1 (3–4 minutes)
The examiner will ask you and your partner some questions. These questions will be about your daily life, interests, likes and dislikes. For example, you may have to speak about school, hobbies or home town.

Part 2 (5–6 minutes)
You and your partner will speak to each other. The examiner will give you a card with some illustrations on it. You will then discuss the activities, things or places illustrated on the card with your partner. The examiner will then ask you and your partner some individual questions about the illustrations on the card.

Test 1

READING AND WRITING (60 minutes)

PART 1

QUESTIONS 1–6

For each question, choose the correct answer.

1

Susie,
Can you take your work stuff out of the living room and put it in your room? Liz is coming for coffee.
Chloe

Chloe wants Susie

A to clean her room.

B to stop working at home.

C to tidy up the living room.

2

STUDENTS!
Cleaners are here every Friday, but please wash up and put things away after you've used the kitchen.
Thank you!

What is this message asking students to do?

A help keep the kitchen tidy at all times

B let the cleaners know when the kitchen's free

C stay out of the kitchen when the cleaners are there

3

Hi Pete,
Could you get me from the train station later tonight? I don't think there'll be any taxis there. Text me back now!
Anna

What does Anna want Pete to do?

A order a taxi to pick her up from the station

B text her when he gets to the station

C give her a lift from the station

4

NEW STUDENTS

Go to Reception to collect your course books before seeing your teacher

A New students should go to Reception before they collect their books.

B Course books will be available at Reception for students.

C Teachers will meet the new students at Reception.

5

Apartment for rent, Redbridge

One double bedroom

Just been painted, with new kitchen

ryt@ukmail.com

A This flat is in a new building.

B This flat is ready to move into.

C This flat is too small for two people.

6

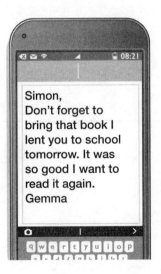

Simon,
Don't forget to bring that book I lent you to school tomorrow. It was so good I want to read it again.
Gemma

Why did Gemma contact Simon?

A to tell him about a book she liked

B to ask him to return her book

C to offer to lend him a book

PART 2

QUESTIONS 7–13

For each question, choose the correct answer.

		Sandy Bay	High Wood	Black Lake
7	Which campsite has an indoor swimming pool?	A	B	C
8	Which campsite offers water sports classes?	A	B	C
9	Which campsite has great views?	A	B	C
10	Which campsite has a shop where people can buy food?	A	B	C
11	Which campsite offers evening activities?	A	B	C
12	Which campsite has lots of space for your tent?	A	B	C
13	Which campsite has bikes you can borrow?	A	B	C

Three great campsites to try this summer

Sandy Bay
This campsite is on an excellent beach, and has its own surfing school with special prices for campers. You can also learn to windsurf and sail there. The sea is safe for swimming, so it's a great place for families. The large swimming pool is great in summer, and has a wide area of grass around it. Its small supermarket has long opening hours. It doesn't matter what size tent you bring, as the campsite is large and you won't be too near your neighbours!

High Wood
There are lots of activities you can do at High Wood campsite, from fishing to cycling, and they'll lend you any of the equipment you need. It's not as large as some campsites, but it's clean and modern. It has a fantastic pool with a roof window which can open and close. There's also a special area where you can watch films or dance under the stars to local bands. For food shopping, try the shop in the nearby village.

Black Lake
The wonderful thing about Black Lake campsite is waking up in the morning and seeing the beautiful mountains all around you. You don't have to bring your own tent – there are some already there you can pay to use. There's lots to do – you can swim in the lake or walk in the forest. And don't forget to bring your mountain bike with you! If you want to cook for yourself, the shop in the next village has a good variety of food.

PART 3

QUESTIONS 14–18

For each question, choose the correct answer.

Jack Calder

Violin player Jack Calder plays in the Australian band, Ocean Blue.

Jack Calder started playing the violin when he was ten. 'My music teacher played and one day he asked if anyone wanted to learn. Some girls put up their hands and so did I. I didn't have a violin, but my uncle said I could use his. The lessons were really hard at first, but playing the violin soon became important to me.'

After leaving school, Jack moved to Melbourne. For a time, he preferred listening to music to playing it. The rock music he listened to sounded very different from violin music, so he bought an electric violin, and started putting the things he liked about rock music into the music he played on his violin.

A year later, Jack met a small group of Melbourne musicians. 'We all thought about music in the same way and started Ocean Blue together. A year later, we were playing lots of concerts, and our music was selling well. But we didn't want this to make us different people. We didn't want to stop being friends.'

Jack meets many people who think playing the violin is an unusual career, but he doesn't agree with them. 'I think it's the best thing in the world. I guess I'm lucky that way. The internet has changed music, but when I walk into a violin shop it's like entering another world – one where time has stopped. Someone has looked after these beautiful old instruments that are two or three hundred years old. I think that's amazing.'

---

14   What do we learn about Jack in the first paragraph?

    A   He was the only person at school to play the violin.

    B   He learned to play on an instrument that he borrowed.

    C   He enjoyed playing the violin as soon as he started learning.

15   What is the writer doing in the second paragraph?

    A   explaining why Jack thought some music was easy to play

    B   saying why only a few people liked the music Jack played

    C   describing how Jack changed the kind of music he played

16   What does Jack say about Ocean Blue?

    A   Nobody in the band liked travelling far to play in a concert.

    B   The band members were interested in different kinds of music.

    C   Everyone wanted to stay friends when the band became successful.

17   Why does Jack think he is lucky?

    A   He meets lots of people.

    B   He loves what he does.

    C   He has an unusual career.

18   Jack thinks it is a good idea

    A   to keep some things that people used in the past.

    B   to make more music available on the internet.

    C   to teach more people to play an instrument.

PART 4

QUESTIONS 19–24

For each question, choose the correct answer.

The London Marathon

In 1979, two British men called John Disley and Chris Brasher **(19)** .... to run the New York Marathon. This 42-kilometre race goes through the city, past many of its famous tourist sights. Disley and Brasher found that it was very different from marathons in the UK.

At that **(20)** .... in the UK, nobody was interested in marathons, but in New York, there were large **(21)** .... of people watching. Afterwards, the two men had the **(22)** .... of starting a similar race in London.

The first London Marathon was in 1981, and over six thousand runners **(23)** .... part. Since then, the race has happened every year, and has become popular with runners from all over the world. Over a million people have completed it, and it is **(24)** .... on TV in nearly 200 countries.

19	**A**	thought	**B**	said	**C**	decided
20	**A**	year	**B**	day	**C**	time
21	**A**	members	**B**	crowds	**C**	visitors
22	**A**	idea	**B**	answer	**C**	fact
23	**A**	stayed	**B**	took	**C**	made
24	**A**	shown	**B**	made	**C**	held

PART 5

QUESTIONS 25–30

For each question, write the correct answer.
Write **ONE** word for each gap.

Example:

0	*to*

Welcome **(0)** .... my blog! My name is Mark and I'm 23 years old. I was born in

Australia, but I grew **(25)** .... in France. **(26)** .... the moment, I am working in

Paris, as a photographer for a fashion magazine.

I live near my office and **(27)** .... only takes me ten minutes to get there. Sometimes

I have to travel to other countries to work, **(28)** .... example, last month I went to

(29) .... USA to take photos at a big fashion show.

I get to meet a lot of very interesting people. Leave me a message **(30)** .... you want

to ask me any questions.

PART 6

QUESTION 31

You took part in a sports competition at the weekend.
Write an email to your English friend, Robbie.

In your email:

- say which sport the competition was for

- explain how you felt at the start of the competition

- say how well you did in the competition.

Write **25 words** or more.

Write the email on your answer sheet.

PART 7

QUESTION 32

Look at the three pictures.
Write the story shown in the pictures.
Write **35 words** or more.

Write the story on your answer sheet.

LISTENING (approximately 30 minutes)

PART 1

QUESTIONS 1–5

For each question, choose the correct answer.

1 How did the woman travel to work this morning?

  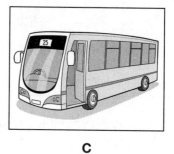

| A | B | C |

2 What will the man eat first at the restaurant?

 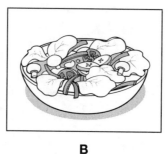 

| A | B | C |

3 Which was the view from the woman's hotel room?

| A | B | C |

4 Why will the man miss the concert tonight?

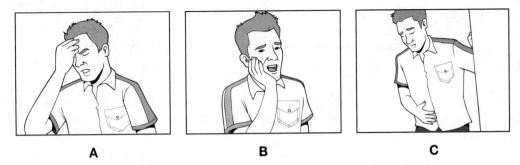

A   B   C

5 What will the woman wear for the party?

A   B   C

PART 2

QUESTIONS 6–10

For each question, write the correct answer in the gap.
Write **one word** or a **number** or a **date** or a **time**.

You will hear a man giving information about a city bus tour.

City Bus Tours

Name of guide:	*Greg*
Time last tour starts:	(6) .... p.m.
Colour of tour bus stop:	(7) ....
Length of tour:	(8) .... minutes
Where to use ticket for discount:	(9) ....
Place tour ends:	(10) ....

PART 3

QUESTIONS 11–15

For each question, choose the correct answer.

You will hear two friends, Richard and Barbara, talking about a new supermarket.

11   What surprised Richard when he went to the supermarket?

    A   its size

    B   the time it opens

    C   the number of people there

12   This week, there are discounts on

    A   meat.

    B   fruit.

    C   vegetables.

13   What did Richard like most about the supermarket?

    A   the café

    B   the staff

    C   the music

14   What problem did Richard have at the supermarket?

    A   He didn't have any cash.

    B   He had to wait before he could pay.

    C   He couldn't use his credit card.

15   What does Barbara say about the car park?

    A   It's only for customers.

    B   It's quite far from the entrance.

    C   It's difficult to find.

PART 4

QUESTIONS 16–20

For each question, choose the correct answer.

---

16 You will hear a woman talking on the radio about her job.
What's her job?

A engineer

B mechanic

C pilot

17 You will hear a woman talking to a friend about a film.
What does she say about the film?

A It was funny.

B It was true.

C It was scary.

18 You will hear a sports coach talking to some footballers.
What would the coach like them to become better at?

A running with the ball

B getting goals

C working as a team

19 You will hear two friends talking about a website.
Why does Julia prefer to buy clothes from the website?

A It offers the latest fashions.

B The discounts are excellent.

C Orders always arrive quickly.

20 You will hear two colleagues talking together.
Why was the man not at the meeting this morning?

A He had to go to the dentist.

B He had other work to do.

C He wasn't feeling well.

PART 5

QUESTIONS 21–25

For each question, choose the correct answer.

You will hear Gregory talking to Angelika about some things he has bought for his new house. What is he going to put in each place?

Example:

0   garden   H

Places

21	dining room	
22	bathroom	
23	bedroom	
24	living room	
25	kitchen	

Things

A   bookcase

B   clock

C   cupboard

D   curtains

E   lamp

F   mirror

G   seat

H   table

You now have 6 minutes to write your answers on the answer sheet.

Test 2

READING AND WRITING (60 minutes)

PART 1

QUESTIONS 1–6

For each question, choose the correct answer.

1

From: Cristina
To: Molly

Sorry, but I'm going to be late for our meeting about the new football team tomorrow. I'll probably arrive around 10.20 – start without me!

A Cristina says she might miss the meeting tomorrow.

B Cristina wants to change the time of tomorrow's meeting.

C Cristina is telling Molly not to wait for her tomorrow.

2

Sam's Café
Open daily: 6.00 a.m. – 3.00 p.m.
20% student discount:
6.00 a.m. – 10.00 a.m.

A The café is closed to students after 10 a.m.

B Students who come early get lower prices.

C Students cannot eat lunch here every day.

3

Tess.
Could I borrow your laptop tonight? Mine's at the computer repair shop. If not, do you know anyone who can lend me one?
Missie

A Missie is asking Tess to help her find a laptop to use.

B Missie is offering to lend her laptop to a friend.

C Missie wants to find someone to repair her laptop.

4

> # SPECIAL OFFER UNTIL SATURDAY
>
> ## Shirts £10 each when you buy two!
>
> ## Usual price £25

A This Saturday each shirt will cost £10 less than usual.

B If you buy more than one shirt, you can save money.

C After Saturday, the price of these shirts will go down.

5

Matt,
We're already at the cinema but can't see you anywhere. The film starts soon and Ben wants to get some snacks.
Hurry up!
Dom

Why did Dom send this message?

A He is worried they'll miss some of the film.

B He wants to eat something before the film.

C He needs to tell Matt where the cinema is.

6

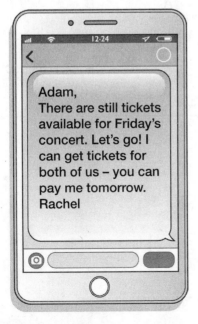

Adam,
There are still tickets available for Friday's concert. Let's go! I can get tickets for both of us – you can pay me tomorrow.
Rachel

Why did Rachel send this message?

A to offer to buy a concert ticket for Adam

B to find out more about the concert from Adam

C to tell Adam what the concert tickets cost

PART 2

QUESTIONS 7–13

For each question, choose the correct answer.

		Petra	**Bea**	**Sara**
7	Who didn't enjoy tennis as much as other activities at the tennis centre?	A	B	C
8	Who had to change her plans for the future after an accident?	A	B	C
9	Who says she missed people from home while she was at the tennis centre?	A	B	C
10	Who went back to the tennis centre to learn to become a coach?	A	B	C
11	Who doesn't like the idea of travelling a lot for her job?	A	B	C
12	Who moved to a different country with a member of her family?	A	B	C
13	Who teaches tennis to young people who haven't played before?	A	B	C

How I became a tennis coach

Petra

I grew up in Germany, but when I was 17, I moved to Spain so I could go to a tennis centre there. It was hard to be without my family and friends, especially when I hurt myself or got ill. However, my tennis improved a lot. After three years, I left the centre and began my career. I started playing in big competitions around the world. I did OK, but wasn't earning enough money, so I quickly decided to become a tennis coach instead. I now teach children who are just starting the game, which is fun.

Bea

When I was 14, my dad sent me to a tennis centre near my home in Italy. He thought I might become a top player like him, but I saw how much time he spent going from one country to another during his career, and I've never wanted that for myself. My favourite things at the tennis centre were spending time at the pool or having barbecues with friends in the evenings. I'm now a coach, and teach young tennis stars at summer camps in Italy.

Sara

When I went to live in Spain so I could go to a famous tennis centre there, my dad came with me, and my mum stayed at home in Scotland. My tennis really improved during my two years there, but when I broke my foot it became clear that a career as a tennis player wasn't going to be possible. I went home for a year and then returned to the centre to do a coaching course. I now teach the best young players in Scotland.

PART 3

QUESTIONS 14–18

For each question, choose the correct answer.

Joining a ballroom dancing club

By Pippa Cartwright

When I started college, I wanted to find a club to join. One of the first ones I looked at was ballroom dancing – a type of dance you do with a partner. The people there seemed to be having a great time, and it didn't cost much, so I decided to join.

The first week I went, I was really worried because the teacher told us that there were nineteen different dances we had to learn. But it's been fine. When there's a new thing to learn, he shows it to us lots of times and makes sure we're all good at it before we do the next thing.

When I joined, I didn't know any of the other people in the club because we all study different subjects. But it's been a great way to meet people, and I've made some of my best friends in the club.

One of the reasons we learn the dances is to enter competitions. I couldn't wait to do my first one. Before we started, I was a bit worried. But during the competition, my partner and I remembered everything about our dances. We were great. We didn't win any prizes, but it didn't matter – we loved it!

Joining the ballroom dancing club has been fantastic. In the past, I always did the same sports and activities, year after year, but ballroom dancing has taught me there's nothing scary about doing something you've never tried before. I still do lots of sports, but now I can add ballroom dancing to my list of hobbies.

---

14   Why did Pippa join the dance club?

    A   She thought it looked fun.

    B   She didn't have to pay for it.

    C   She didn't like any of the other clubs.

15   What does Pippa say about the dance teacher?

    A   He teaches them a new dance every week.

    B   He often tells new members how good they are.

    C   He repeats new things until everyone can do them.

16   What does Pippa say about the other club members?

    A   She has become close to some of them.

    B   She is on the same course as some of them.

    C   She was friends with some of them before joining.

17   How did Pippa feel about her first dance competition?

    A   happy to win first prize

    B   upset that she forgot the dances

    C   excited to take part

18   In the final paragraph, Pippa says

    A   ballroom dancing is her favourite hobby.

    B   she's learned not to be afraid to do new things.

    C   she isn't sure which activity to try next.

PART 4

QUESTIONS 19–24

For each question, choose the correct answer.

Walter Bonatti

Walter Bonatti, one of the greatest alpine mountain climbers of all time, was born in Italy in 1930. As a child, he **(19)** .... his holidays in Bergamo with his uncles. He loved the mountains there, and at the age of 18, he **(20)** .... to climb the highest and most difficult ones. He was one of the **(21)** .... people to do this and he was very **(22)** .... at it.

He went on to climb many other mountains, including the famous K2 in the Himalayas. At the age of just 35, he decided to **(23)** .... his climbing career. However, he continued to work as a mountain guide and photographer. He also wrote several books about his climbing **(24)** ...., which are read in all Italian schools.

19	A	travelled	B	went	C	spent
20	A	became	B	began	C	turned
21	A	early	B	first	C	soon
22	A	successful	B	interested	C	popular
23	A	shut	B	close	C	end
24	A	experiences	B	occupations	C	subjects

PART 5

QUESTIONS 25–30

For each question, write the correct answer.
Write **ONE** word for each gap.

Example:

0	*at*

From:	Bea
To:	Tania

How are things? Are you busy **(0)** .... the moment? **(25)** .... you remember our

conversation last weekend about going **(26)** .... the theatre? Well, the play 'Fathers and

Sons' **(27)** .... showing next week at West Theatre. Shall **(28)** .... go and see it

together? I've heard it's very good!

From:	Tania
To:	Bea

That sounds great! **(29)** .... would you like to go? I'm busy on Friday next week,

(30) .... I'm free the other days. Shall I get the tickets? I can buy them online. We've

both got student ID cards, so they won't be too expensive.

PART 6

QUESTION 31

Read the email from your English friend, Pat.

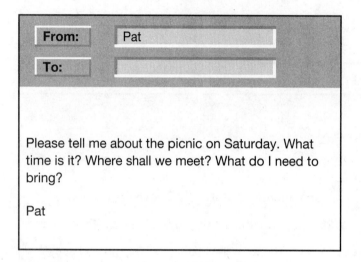

From: Pat

To:

Please tell me about the picnic on Saturday. What time is it? Where shall we meet? What do I need to bring?

Pat

Write an email to Pat and answer the questions.
Write **25 words** or more.

Write the email on your answer sheet.

PART 7

QUESTION 32

Look at the three pictures.
Write the story shown in the pictures.
Write **35 words** or more.

Write the story on your answer sheet.

LISTENING (approximately 30 minutes)

PART 1

QUESTIONS 1–5

For each question, choose the correct answer.

---

1 Where is the cup now?

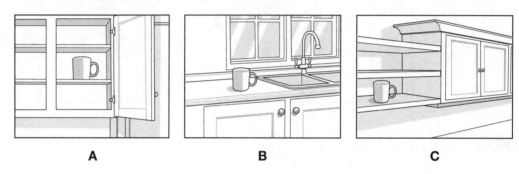

A   B   C

2 Who will Sally meet at the station?

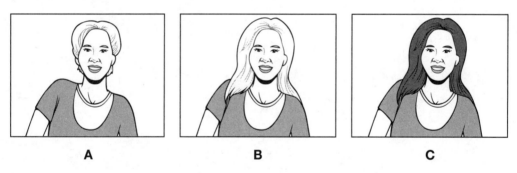

A   B   C

3 What did the man learn to do at the beach?

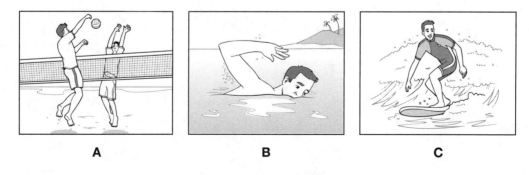

A   B   C

4   Where are they going to meet?

A   B   C

5   What didn't the man buy?

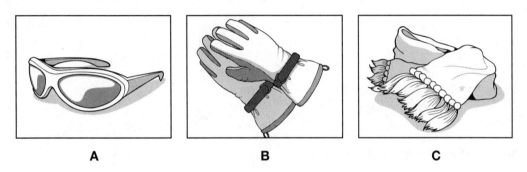

A   B   C

PART 2

QUESTIONS 6–10

For each question, write the correct answer in the gap.
Write **one word** or a **number** or a **date** or a **time**.

You will hear a woman talking to sailing club members about a trip.

Sailing club trip

Date:	19th July
Time to arrive back at club:	**(6)** .... p.m.
Name of café for lunch:	**(7)** ....
Bring:	**(8)** ....
Number of people:	**(9)** ....
Secretary's name:	**(10)** Ms ....

PART 3

QUESTIONS 11–15

For each question, choose the correct answer.

You will hear a manager, Victoria, talking to her assistant, Daniel, about the new company building.

11 How will staff find out about the new building?

   A   in an email

   B   at a meeting

   C   at a company meal

12 Why is the company moving to a new building?

   A   to save money

   B   to be in the town centre

   C   to have larger offices

13 When will staff start working in the new building?

   A   the end of May

   B   the beginning of July

   C   the middle of August

14 What does Daniel think the staff will enjoy most about the new area?

   A   the restaurants

   B   the shops

   C   the gym

15 What does Daniel need to order next?

   A   keys

   B   signs

   C   furniture

PART 4

QUESTIONS 16–20

For each question, choose the correct answer.

16 You will hear a woman, Jen, telling her friend about her favourite singer, Mikey.
What's just happened?

   A   Jen's seen him on stage.

   B   Jen's taken a photo of him.

   C   Jen's had a conversation with him.

17 You will hear a man, Alex, talking to a friend about a tennis competition.
Why didn't Alex do well in the competition?

   A   He was thirsty.

   B   He was hungry.

   C   He was tired.

18 You will hear two people talking at a tourist information centre.
What advice does the man give the woman?

   A   Don't miss a special exhibition.

   B   Don't visit the museum today.

   C   Don't buy tickets too late.

19 You will hear two friends talking about what they did at the weekend.
What didn't the woman do at the weekend?

   A   watch TV

   B   play sport

   C   go shopping

20 You will hear a man talking to his friend about his new flat.
What's he going to do now?

   A   paint the flat

   B   turn the heating on

   C   move some furniture

PART 5

QUESTIONS 21–25

For each question, choose the correct answer.

You will hear a woman telling her brother about her friends and their hobbies.
What hobby does each friend have?

Example:

0	Simon	**B**

Friends

21	Jane	☐
22	Derek	☐
23	Mary	☐
24	Tony	☐
25	Sarah	☐

Hobbies

A	acting
B	art
C	cycling
D	making music
E	photography
F	reading
G	travelling
H	watching sport

You now have 6 minutes to write your answers on the answer sheet.

Test 3

READING AND WRITING (60 minutes)

PART 1

QUESTIONS 1–6

For each question, choose the correct answer.

1

> **Swimming pool closed for building work**
>
> **Open from Tuesday for lessons only**

A People who have swimming classes can go on Tuesday.

B The pool will be closed to all customers after Tuesday.

C Swimming lessons will be in a new pool on Tuesday.

2

> **Chess club members!**
>
> We're meeting in the library this Wednesday instead of the hall, as there's a dance show happening there at 7 p.m.

The chess club is

A on a different day this week.

B in a different place this week.

C at a different time this week.

3

> Rob,
> Leave your laptop in the kitchen before you go out and I'll see if I can find out why it's not working.
> Dad

Why did Rob's dad write this note?

A to ask if he can use Rob's laptop

B to tell Rob where he left his laptop

C to offer to check Rob's laptop

4

Mark,
I have to work until 6.00, so I can't meet you at the café. See you at the cinema instead, just before the film.
Rafa

A Rafa needs to change the plans for this evening.

B Rafa will eat at work before going to the cinema.

C Rafa prefers to see the film at a later time.

5

Sightseeing trips twice daily

Buses – 9.00 a.m. & 2.00 p.m.

Tickets only available from tourist office

A It's not possible to buy tickets on the bus.

B Tourists must book both trips at 9.00 a.m.

C Each sightseeing trip takes two hours.

6

Cinema park is full
Please use the free one in the shopping centre

A You should pay for cinema parking in the shopping centre.

B People who want to see a film must drive to the shopping centre cinema.

C Cinema visitors should use a different car park.

PART 2

QUESTIONS 7–13

For each question, choose the correct answer.

		Paula	Sally	Kim
7	Who does her hobby with people in her family?	A	B	C
8	Who started classes after getting some good advice?	A	B	C
9	Who began her hobby after feeling unhappy at work?	A	B	C
10	Who did her hobby for a long time before starting classes?	A	B	C
11	Who has made new friends at her classes?	A	B	C
12	Who felt worried before starting her classes?	A	B	C
13	Who first had classes in her hobby as a child?	A	B	C

Learning for fun

Meet three women who enjoy taking classes in their free time.

Paula

I work full time as a nurse, and don't have much time for hobbies, but I've been interested in photography since I was a child. On my last holiday to India, I took lots of pictures, and everyone I showed them to said they were great. So I decided to do a course. At first, I was afraid I might not be good enough. After all, it was my first time as a student for ten years! But I loved it from the very first lesson.

Sally

When I was still at school, I started learning the violin. It was fun and I was quite good at it, but I didn't do it for long, because I had so many other hobbies. Then last year, I was having a hard time in my job, and my husband bought me a violin as a present. I started learning with a teacher again. All three of my children are learning to play instruments too, so now we can practise with each other!

Kim

Last year I moved to a new city because of my job. I didn't have anything to do in the evenings, so one of my colleagues said I should try a class at the local college. I immediately thought of cooking. My mum was a fantastic cook, and when I was a child I loved watching her in the kitchen, but I never learned how to cook myself. The other students on the course are around my age, and sometimes we go to restaurants together, or even the cinema.

PART 3

QUESTIONS 14–18

For each question, choose the correct answer.

My city

Pop singer Charlotte Bond talks about living in London.

I live in the centre of London. I love it because there's always something happening and there are people around whatever time it is. Famous people like it too – they often come here for the restaurants and shops.

I've lived here all my life. When I was little, I had singing lessons at a place near where I live now. I was afraid of the teacher at first, and some of the songs we did together were quite hard to learn. But she was good at what she did and I learned a lot of things that have helped me in my career.

When friends visit me now, I enjoy taking them sightseeing. You can get a bus around the city, but we prefer to walk. I've got a little car and I love driving, but there's so much traffic here, and it's hard to find parking spaces.

One building I love is the Natural History Museum. They sometimes hold parties there, and last December my band and I played at one. I'll never forget it. When I go to exhibitions at the museum with my friends, I tell them all about that night and how amazing it was.

Soon I'll be leaving London to go on tour with my band. We're playing in lots of new cities and I can't wait to explore them. We've sold lots of tickets, which is great. I'll be away from my family for six months, but they're coming to see me sing, so it's fine.

---

14 What does Charlotte love about the centre of London?

    A It is always busy.

    B Famous people often visit.

    C The shops are very good.

15 How does Charlotte feel about the singing lessons she had?

    A She's surprised she can remember them.

    B She's sorry she didn't try harder.

    C She's glad she did them.

16 What does Charlotte think is the best way to see the city?

    A by car

    B on foot

    C by bus

17 Why does Charlotte love the Natural History Museum?

    A She had a special experience there.

    B She thinks the building is beautiful.

    C She enjoys visiting the exhibitions.

18 What does Charlotte say about going on tour with her band?

    A She hopes lots of people will buy tickets for her shows.

    B She feels excited about seeing new places.

    C She's worried she'll miss her family.

PART 4

QUESTIONS 19–24

For each question, choose the correct answer.

Camels

Camels are one of the only large animals that can live happily in the Sahara Desert. The hot weather and strong winds are not a **(19)** .... for them. Also, they do not need to eat or drink every day, and this **(20)** .... them very useful to the people who live there.

Camels begin working at the age of about four years old and don't stop until they are around 25 to 30. They can carry people or things a very long **(21)** .... , and because of this they are sometimes **(22)** .... the 'ships of the desert'.

These days, there are roads across some **(23)** .... of the Sahara, so buses and lorries are often **(24)** .... However, in places where there are no roads, camels are still the only type of transport.

---

19   **A**   trouble   **B**   mistake   **C**   problem

20   **A**   gets   **B**   has   **C**   makes

21   **A**   way   **B**   path   **C**   road

22   **A**   described   **B**   said   **C**   called

23   **A**   parts   **B**   examples   **C**   things

24   **A**   put   **B**   used   **C**   done

PART 5

QUESTIONS 25–30

For each question, write the correct answer.

Write **ONE** word for each gap.

Example: | **0** | *hope* |

| **From:** | Jenny |
| **To:** | David |

Hi David,

I **(0)** .... you're well. It's my brother Tom's birthday **(25)** .... month, and I don't know **(26)** .... to buy him for a present. Have you got **(27)** .... ideas? He's the same age **(28)** .... you, and likes the same kind of things.

Thanks,

Jenny

| **From:** | David |
| **To:** | Jenny |

Hi Jenny,

I think I can help you! Why not get Tom a book? I've just read *Dragon Teeth*, which was written **(29)** .... Michael Crichton. He's such a fantastic author! I loved it, and I think **(30)** .... brother would like it too.

David

PART 6

QUESTION 31

Read the email from your English friend, Alex.

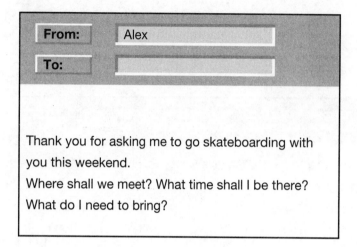

From:	Alex
To:	

Thank you for asking me to go skateboarding with you this weekend.
Where shall we meet? What time shall I be there?
What do I need to bring?

Write an email to Alex and answer the questions.
Write **25 words** or more.

Write the email on your answer sheet.

PART 7

QUESTION 32

Look at the three pictures.

Write the story shown in the pictures.

Write **35 words** or more.

Write the story on your answer sheet.

LISTENING (approximately 30 minutes)

PART 1

QUESTIONS 1–5

For each question, choose the correct answer.

---

1 Where will they go if it rains tomorrow?

A   B   C

2 Why didn't the woman buy the book?

A   B   C

3 Where does the man work now?

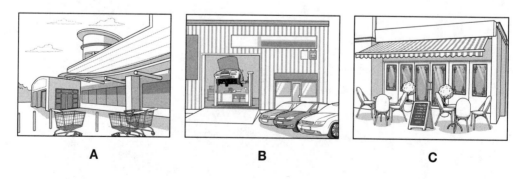

A   B   C

4 Where does the man want to go?

A   **B**   **C**

5 What's the man making?

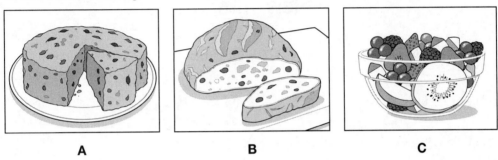

A   **B**   **C**

PART 2

QUESTIONS 6–10

For each question, write the correct answer in the gap.
Write **one word** or **a number** or **a date** or **a time**.

You will hear a man talking about a film on local radio.

New film

Name of film: Runner

Subject of film: (6) ....

Name of cinema: (7) ....

Start date: (8) ....

Start time: (9) .... p.m.

Cost of student ticket: (10) £.................................

PART 3

QUESTIONS 11–15

For each question, choose the correct answer.

You will hear Phil talking to his friend Jess about a new sports centre.

11 How did Jess find out about the new sports centre?

A She saw a poster.

B A friend of hers works there.

C She heard about it on the radio.

12 What doesn't Phil like about the sports centre?

A It's too noisy.

B It's very expensive.

C It's not big enough.

13 Phil prefers to go to the sports centre

A early in the morning.

B at the weekend.

C during working hours.

14 Why is the new swimming pool closed at the moment?

A They are cleaning it.

B There's a competition.

C The water's cold.

15 Members of the sports centre

A should buy special shoes.

B can get a discount in the café.

C needn't pay for exercise classes.

PART 4

QUESTIONS 16–20

For each question, choose the correct answer.

16 You will hear a woman talking to a friend about getting to work.
    Why did the woman arrive at the office late?

    A   The road was closed.

    B   There was a problem with her car.

    C   She couldn't find her car keys.

17 You will hear a man, Peter, talking to a friend about his plans.
    Where will Peter be this Saturday?

    A   at a party

    B   in another country

    C   on a boat

18 You will hear a man talking about a music festival.
    What's different about the festival this year?

    A   how long it is

    B   where it is

    C   when it is

19 You will hear two people talking about their school days.
    Which subject did they both enjoy at school?

    A   history

    B   geography

    C   science

20 You will hear someone speaking to customers in a supermarket.
    What's cheaper in the supermarket this week?

    A   desserts

    B   soft drinks

    C   fruit

PART 5

QUESTIONS 21–25

For each question, choose the correct answer.

You will hear Helena talking to her friend Steve about hotels in their city.
What does Steve think about each hotel?

Example:

0	Plaza Hotel	E

Hotels			**Opinions**	
21	City Hotel	☐	A	comfortable beds
			B	expensive
22	The Bridge Hotel	☐	C	friendly staff
23	Lemontree Hotel	☐	D	good food
			E	hard to find
24	Greenleaf Hotel	☐	F	large bedrooms
			G	no parking
25	The International Hotel	☐	H	noisy

You now have 6 minutes to write your answers on the answer sheet.

Test 4

READING AND WRITING (60 minutes)

PART 1

QUESTIONS 1–6

For each question, choose the correct answer.

1

From: Jack
To: Football coach

I'm at the dentist's, so I won't be at football practice at 4 o'clock. I can get there for 4.30 – sorry.

A Jack doesn't want to go to football practice today.

B Jack won't be on time for today's football practice.

C Jack can't go to football practice today because he's at the dentist's.

2

Ollie,
I was late this morning, so I took your bike to go to college. I'll be back at 4 o'clock. I hope that's OK?
Leo

Leo wrote this message

A to ask Ollie what time they need to do something.

B to thank Ollie for doing something for him.

C to explain to Ollie why he has done something.

3

> ## Castle Restaurant
> These outside tables are for restaurant customers only
> Picnic tables by lake

A People must buy their food and drinks inside before they choose a table.

B People may sit here if they are eating food bought in this place.

C If you have brought your own sandwiches, you can eat them here.

4

College Clubs
Please see college website for details of all free clubs this term. Book online or speak to college secretary before Friday.

A Students can check the cost of joining a club by going online.

B Students must decide what they want to do by the end of the week.

C Students must not book a club before speaking to the college secretary.

5

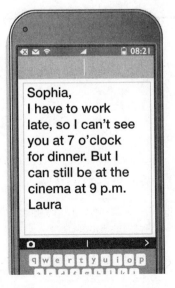

Weekend music festival

This entrance for people with tickets

Tickets for Sunday available online

A If you don't have a ticket, you can't get in here.

B If you want a ticket for Sunday, you must wait here.

C If you go to another entrance, you can get a ticket.

6

08:21

Sophia,
I have to work late, so I can't see you at 7 o'clock for dinner. But I can still be at the cinema at 9 p.m.
Laura

Why did Laura write this message?

A to invite Sophia to see a film with her

B to check when she needs to meet Sophia

C to let Sophia know about a change of plan

PART 2

QUESTIONS 7–13

For each question, choose the correct answer.

		Priya	Zoe	Heike
7	Who practises her dancing seven days a week?	A	B	C
8	Who feels scared before she goes on stage?	A	B	C
9	Who would like to try a different type of dance?	A	B	C
10	Who feels sad that she can't spend much time with her friends?	A	B	C
11	Who says she has no plans to change her job?	A	B	C
12	Who has a family member who is famous?	A	B	C
13	Who says the people she dances with are older than her?	A	B	C

A dancer's life

Priya

I work as a dancer, and I'm also studying part-time. I practise most days and have to do my college work, so I can't always go out with my friends at weekends, but that's fine. We text each other every day. I mostly dance in musicals, but in the future I'm hoping to start jazz dance. My mum always comes to watch me on stage. She's my biggest fan! Being a dancer isn't easy, but I want to do it as long as I can.

Zoe

There are dancers of all ages in my dance company and every year we go on international tours together. My cousin also dances with me. She's been a dancer for seven years and people everywhere know her now. She was a jazz dancer in the past, but loves what we do now. I don't usually feel worried before I dance in front of others – I know I'm good! But that's only because I try so hard. I spend about three hours dancing every day.

Heike

I come from a family of dancers so maybe it's not surprising I'm one too. I'm in a hip-hop group at the moment, but actually I can dance to any music – even jazz! I'm the youngest member of my dance group. Before each show, I think of everything that might go wrong, but I try hard to tell myself it'll all be OK. We dance all over the country, so I'm away from home almost every day and I miss my friends a lot.

PART 3

QUESTIONS 14–18

For each question, choose the correct answer.

Travel writer

Tim Greenwood lives in Oakland, USA. He has written about Cambodia, Thailand and India. At the moment he is writing a book about Nepal.

Tim, how did you start travelling?
We never travelled as a family, but when I was a teenager I saw movies like *Lawrence of Arabia* and they made me want to travel. I left college at the age of 21 and went to Europe alone. That trip didn't go well – I was too young and didn't know how to look after myself.

How did you start writing?
I've loved writing since I was ten – I've never wanted any other career. At 21, I wrote for my weekly college paper and then started writing travel articles. At first, none of the travel magazines I sent them to wanted to buy them, but that slowly changed. It took two or three years, I guess.

What do you find difficult about writing?
It is easy to spend all my time travelling and then not have time to open up my laptop and work! Also, it's hard to earn enough money. I'll never stop writing, but one day I may have to do a few hours a week teaching just to pay the bills.

What's the best thing about being a travel writer?
I get letters from young people who've read my books and articles and enjoy my work. I just love that!

---

14 As a teenager, Tim

    A   went on trips with his parents.

    B   became interested in seeing the world.

    C   spent too much time watching TV.

15 What does Tim say about his trip to Europe?

    A   He didn't have time to see everything.

    B   It was more fun than college.

    C   It was not a great success.

16 When Tim was 21, he couldn't

    A   travel as much as he wanted to.

    B   decide what to write about.

    C   sell many of his articles.

17 In the future, Tim thinks he might

    A   do some extra work.

    B   earn more from writing.

    C   change his job.

18 What does Tim like about being a travel writer?

    A   hearing from his fans

    B   giving advice to people

    C   meeting other young writers

PART 4

QUESTIONS 19–24

For each question, choose the correct answer.

An unusual holiday

Most people go on holiday to get away from work. But in the beautiful Scottish village of

Wigtown, it's **(19)** .... to rent a flat above a bookshop, and work as the **(20)** ....

of the bookshop for a week. This holiday is very popular with people who love books and who

have always **(21)** .... their own bookshop.

However, this is a holiday, so people staying there don't have to work very hard. They can

(22) .... the opening hours of the shop, and they just have a few jobs to do, such as

(23) .... the shelves with books.

Guests also get a bike, so they can **(24)** .... the area when the shop is closed. The

holiday is so popular that the flat is fully booked for the next three years.

---

19   **A**   able   **B**   possible   **C**   available

20   **A**   manager   **B**   colleague   **C**   customer

21   **A**   hoped   **B**   wanted   **C**   decided

22   **A**   think   **B**   find   **C**   choose

23   **A**   putting   **B**   adding   **C**   filling

24   **A**   look   **B**   ride   **C**   explore

PART 5

QUESTIONS 25–30

For each question, write the correct answer.

Write **ONE** word for each gap.

Example: | **0** | *with* |

From: Cara

To: Ashley

I'm in Ireland staying **(0)** .... with my friend and we're having a great holiday. My friend's

house is near the sea, so we can **(25)** .... swimming every day, and there are

lots of other things to do as well. Yesterday we rode horses on the beach and had

(26) .... lovely picnic in the mountains.

How are you? **(27)** .... you been on holiday yet? I'll be back home at the weekend.

(28) .... you want to go to the cinema **(29)** .... week? There's a new film I really

want to see. Please **(30)** .... me know.

PART 6

QUESTION 31

You want to go to the shopping centre on Saturday with your English friend, Alex.
Write an email to Alex.

In your email:

- ask Alex to go to the shopping centre with you on Saturday

- say what you need to buy

- explain how you will travel there.

Write **25 words** or more.

Write the email on your answer sheet.

PART 7

QUESTION 32

Look at the three pictures.

Write the story shown in the pictures.

Write **35 words** or more.

Write the story on your answer sheet.

LISTENING (approximately 30 minutes)

PART 1

QUESTIONS 1–5

For each question, choose the correct answer.

---

1 What was the weather like for the football match?

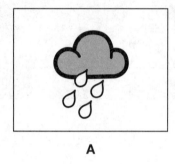

A   **B**   **C**

2 What sport is the woman going to start doing soon?

A   **B**   **C**

3 Why was the man late for work?

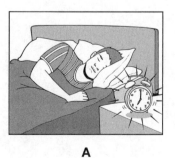

A   **B**   **C**

4   Which food is the man eating?

A   B   C

5   What has the man had problems with?

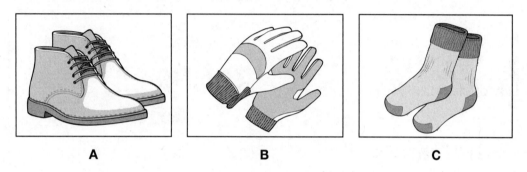

A   B   C

PART 2

QUESTIONS 6–10

For each question, write the correct answer in the gap.
Write **one word** or a **number** or a **date** or a **time**.

You will hear some information about music classes at a local college.

Music classes

Musical instrument: guitar

Day of class: **(6)** ....

Time class starts: **(7)** .... p.m.

Room for beginners' class: **(8)** ....

Teacher's name: **(9)** Mrs ....

Month of rock concert: **(10)** ....

PART 3

QUESTIONS 11–15

For each question, choose the correct answer.

You will hear a man, Ben, and a woman, Emma, talking about Ben's new flat.

11 When did Ben go to live in his new flat?

    A two days ago

    B two weeks ago

    C two months ago

12 How is Ben's new flat different from his old one?

    A It is nearer to his job.

    B It has better views.

    C It is larger.

13 Which room in the new flat does Ben like best?

    A the bathroom

    B the living room

    C the bedroom

14 What has Emma given Ben for his new flat?

    A shelves

    B carpets

    C curtains

15 Who lives in the flat next to Ben's?

    A a mechanic

    B a journalist

    C a police officer

PART 4

QUESTIONS 16–20

For each question, choose the correct answer.

16 You will hear a man asking for help with his computer.
    What's the problem with it?

   A   The computer won't turn off.

   B   The keyboard isn't working.

   C   The screen isn't bright enough.

17 You will hear a woman talking to her husband.
    Where are they planning to meet the woman's brother?

   A   at the railway station

   B   at the airport

   C   at their home

18 You will hear an explorer talking on the radio.
    What was the last place that he visited?

   A   a mountain

   B   a desert

   C   an island

19 You will hear a man talking to his sister about his new phone.
    Why did he choose this phone?

   A   because it's really light

   B   because it looks modern

   C   because it has a good camera

20 You will hear two colleagues talking about a meeting.
    How do they feel after the meeting?

   A   pleased

   B   worried

   C   tired

PART 5

QUESTIONS 21–25

For each question, choose the correct answer.

You will hear Larry talking to Cara about a friend's birthday.
What present will each person give?

Example:

0	Cara	A

People

21   Anthea   ☐

22   Larry   ☐

23   Kerry   ☐

24   Tony   ☐

25   Hannah   ☐

Presents

A   art equipment

B   bag

C   book

D   chocolate

E   concert ticket

F   jewellery

G   perfume

H   picture

You now have 6 minutes to write your answers on the answer sheet.

Speaking tests

Test 1: Different types of food

Note: The visual materials for Speaking Test 1 appear on page 125.

Part 1 (3–4 minutes)

Phase 1

Interlocutor

To both candidates	Good morning / afternoon / evening. Can I have your mark sheets, please?	
	Hand over the mark sheets to the Assessor.	
	I'm ...., and this is	
To Candidate A	What's your name?	
To Candidate B	And what's your name?	
		Back-up prompts
	B, do you work or are you a student?	Do you work? Do you study? Are you a student?
For UK, ask	Where do you come from?	Are you from (Spain, etc.)?
For non-UK, ask	Where do you live?	Do you live in … (name of district / town etc.)?
	Thank you.	
	A, do you work or are you a student?	Do you work? Do you study? Are you a student?
For UK, ask	Where do you come from?	Are you from (Spain, etc.)?
For non-UK, ask	Where do you live?	Do you live in … (name of district / town etc.)?
	Thank you.	

Phase 2

Interlocutor

Now, let's talk about **the area where you live**.

	Back-up prompts
A, what do you like doing outdoors in your area?	Do you like going to the park in your area?
How do you travel in the area where you live?	Do you travel by bus in the area where you live?
B, where is the best place to go in the evening in your area?	Is the cinema the best place to go in the evening in your area?
What is the traffic like where you live?	Are the roads very busy where you live?

Extended Response
Now, **A**, please tell me something about the people who live near you.

Back-up questions
Do you have many neighbours?
When do you see your neighbours?
Do your friends live near you?

Interlocutor

Now, let's talk about **clothes**.

	Back-up prompts
B, what kind of clothes do you wear when you do sport?	Do you wear trainers when you do sport?
Who do you go shopping for clothes with?	Do you go shopping for clothes with a friend?
A, where do you buy your clothes?	Do you buy your clothes online?
What clothes do you wear when you are at home?	Do you wear jeans when you are at home?

Extended Response
Now, **B**, please tell me something about the clothes you wear when you go to parties.

Back-up questions
Do you wear special clothes when you go to parties?
Do you sometimes buy new clothes for a party?
What colour clothes do you like wearing at parties?

Part 2 (5–6 minutes)

Phase 1

Interlocutor

🕐 *3–4 minutes*

Now, in this part of the test you are going to talk together.

*Place **Part 2** booklet, open at **Test 1**, in front of candidates.*

Here are some pictures that show **different types of food**.

Do you like these different types of food? Say why or why not. I'll say that again.

Do you like these different types of food? Say why or why not.

All right? Now, talk together.

Candidates

....

🕐 *Allow a minimum of 1 minute (maximum of 2 minutes) before moving on to the following questions.*

Interlocutor /
Candidates
Use as appropriate.
Ask each candidate
at least one question.

Do you think ...
... fruit is healthy?
... fast food is expensive?
... cake is nice?
... pizza is popular?
... vegetables are boring?

| *Optional prompt* |
| Why? / Why not? |
| What do **you** think? |

Interlocutor

So, **A**, which of these types of food do you like best?
And you, **B**, which of these types of food do you like best?

Thank you. (Can I have the booklet, please?) *Retrieve **Part 2** booklet.*

Phase 2

Interlocutor
🕐 *Allow up to*
2 minutes

Now, do you prefer having a large meal or just a snack at lunchtime, **B**? (Why?)

And what about you, **A**? (Do you prefer having a large meal or just a snack at lunchtime?) (Why?)

Do you prefer eating inside or outside, **A**? (Why?)

And what about you, **B**? (Do you prefer eating inside or outside?) (Why?)

Thank you. That is the end of the test.

Test 2: Different ways of travelling

Note: The visual materials for Speaking Test 2 appear on page 126.

Part 1 (3–4 minutes)

Phase 1

Interlocutor

To both candidates	Good morning / afternoon / evening. Can I have your mark sheets, please? *Hand over the mark sheets to the Assessor.* I'm ...., and this is ....
To Candidate A	What's your name?
To Candidate B	And what's your name?

		Back-up prompts
	B, do you work or are you a student?	Do you work? Do you study? Are you a student?
For UK, ask	Where do you come from?	Are you from (Spain, etc.)?
For non-UK, ask	Where do you live? Thank you.	Do you live in ... (name of district / town etc.)?
	A, do you work or are you a student?	Do you work? Do you study? Are you a student?
For UK, ask	Where do you come from?	Are you from (Spain, etc.)?
For non-UK, ask	Where do you live? Thank you.	Do you live in ... (name of district / town etc.)?

Phase 2

Interlocutor

Now, let's talk about **sport**.

Back-up prompts

A, what sports do you enjoy watching?

Do you enjoy watching tennis?

What sports can you do near your home?

Can you play football near your home?

B, when do you do sport?

Do you do sport at the weekend?

What sports did you do when you were younger?

Did you play basketball when you were younger?

Extended Response
Now, **A**, please tell me something about a sport you would like to do.

Back-up questions
Why would you like to do this sport?
Can you do this sport indoors or outdoors?
What clothes do people wear to do this sport?

Interlocutor

Now, let's talk about **food**.

Back-up prompts

B, which meal of the day is your favourite?

Is lunch your favourite meal?

How often do you cook?

Do you cook every day?

A, what kind of food do you like to eat?

Do you like to eat pizza?

Who do you usually have dinner with?

Do you usually have dinner with your family?

Extended Response
Now, **B**, please tell me about a place where you like going to eat.

Back-up questions
Why do you like going to this place?
Who do you go to this place with?
When do you go to this place?

Part 2 (5–6 minutes)

Phase 1

Interlocutor
🕐 *3–4 minutes*

Now, in this part of the test you are going to talk together.

*Place **Part 2** booklet, open at **Test 2**, in front of candidates.*

Here are some pictures that show **different ways of travelling**.

Do you like these different ways of travelling? Say why or why not. I'll say that again.

Do you like these different ways of travelling? Say why or why not.

All right? Now, talk together.

Candidates

....

🕐 *Allow a minimum of 1 minute (maximum of 2 minutes) before moving on to the following questions.*

**Interlocutor /
Candidates**
*Use as appropriate.
Ask each candidate
at least one question.*

Do you think …
… flying in a helicopter is exciting?
… riding a horse is dangerous?
… taking a boat is slow?
… taking a taxi is expensive?
… travelling by plane is comfortable?

> *Optional prompt*
> Why? / Why not?
> What do **you** think?

Interlocutor

So, **A**, which of these ways of travelling do you like best?
And you, **B**, which of these ways of travelling do you like best?

Thank you. (Can I have the booklet, please?) *Retrieve **Part 2** booklet.*

Phase 2

Interlocutor
🕐 *Allow up to
2 minutes*

Now, do you prefer long journeys or short journeys, **B**? (Why?)

And what about you, **A**? (Do you prefer long journeys or short journeys?) (Why?)

Which country would you like to visit, **A**? (Why?)

And what about you, **B**? (Which country would you like to visit?) (Why?)

Thank you. That is the end of the test.

Test 3: Different free-time activities

Note: The visual materials for Speaking Test 3 appear on page 127.

Part 1 (3–4 minutes)

Phase 1

Interlocutor

To both candidates	Good morning / afternoon / evening. Can I have your mark sheets, please?	
	Hand over the mark sheets to the Assessor.	
	I'm ...., and this is	
To Candidate A	What's your name?	
To Candidate B	And what's your name?	

		Back-up prompts
	B, do you work or are you a student?	Do you work? Do you study? Are you a student?
For UK, ask	Where do you come from?	Are you from (Spain, etc.)?
For non-UK, ask	Where do you live?	Do you live in … (name of district / town etc.)?
	Thank you.	
	A, do you work or are you a student?	Do you work? Do you study? Are you a student?
For UK, ask	Where do you come from?	Are you from (Spain, etc.)?
For Non-UK, ask	Where do you live?	Do you live in … (name of district / town etc.)?
	Thank you.	

Phase 2

Interlocutor

Now, let's talk about **the weather**.

	Back-up prompts
A, what month of the year is the coldest where you live?	Is it coldest in January where you live?
What do you do when it rains?	Do you read at home when it rains?
B, how often does it snow where you live?	Does it snow once a year where you live?
What is your favourite type of weather?	Do you like hot weather best?

Extended Response
Now, **A**, please tell me something about what you do when the weather is good.

Back-up questions
Who do you spend time with when the weather is good?
Do you eat outside when the weather is good?
How do you feel when the weather is good?

Interlocutor

Now, let's talk about **transport**.

	Back-up prompts
B, how often do you travel by car?	Do you travel by car every day?
Who do you travel to school/university/work with?	Do you travel to school/university/work with friends?
A, how do you get to school/university/work?	Do you get to school/university/work by bus?
Who can ride a bike in your family?	Can you ride a bike?

Extended Response
Now, **B**, please tell me something about transport in the place where you live.

Back-up questions
What type of transport do people use most where you live?
Is there a lot of traffic where you live?
How do people travel at night where you live?

Part 2 (5–6 minutes)

Phase 1

Interlocutor
🕐 *3–4 minutes*

Now, in this part of the test you are going to talk together.

*Place **Part 2** booklet, open at **Test 3**, in front of candidates.*

Here are some pictures that show **different free-time activities**.

Do you like these different free-time activities? Say why or why not. I'll say that again.

Do you like these different free-time activities? Say why or why not.

All right? Now, talk together.

Candidates

....

🕐 *Allow a minimum of 1 minute (maximum of 2 minutes) before moving on to the following questions.*

**Interlocutor /
Candidates**
*Use as appropriate.
Ask each candidate
at least one question.*

Do you think ...
... dancing is exciting?
... listening to music is nice?
... taking photographs is interesting?
... playing the piano is boring?
... riding a bike is fun?

> *Optional prompt*
> Why? / Why not?
> What do **you** think?

Interlocutor

So, **A**, which of these free-time activities do you like best?
And you, **B**, which of these free-time activities do you like best?

Thank you. (Can I have the booklet, please?) *Retrieve **Part 2** booklet.*

Phase 2

Interlocutor
🕐 *Allow up to
2 minutes*

Now, do you enjoy doing free-time activities indoors or outdoors, **B**? (Why?)

And what about you, **A**? (Do you enjoy doing free-time activities indoors or outdoors?) (Why?)

Do you prefer doing hobbies by yourself or with other people, **A**? (Why?)

And what about you, **B**? (Do you prefer doing hobbies by yourself or with other people?) (Why?)

Thank you. That is the end of the test.

Test 4: Different sports

Note: The visual materials for Speaking Test 4 appear on page 128.

Part 1 (3–4 minutes)

Phase 1

Interlocutor

To both candidates	Good morning / afternoon / evening. Can I have your mark sheets, please? *Hand over the mark sheets to the Assessor.* I'm ...., and this is ....
To Candidate A	What's your name?
To Candidate B	And what's your name?

		Back-up prompts
	B, do you work or are you a student?	Do you work? Do you study? Are you a student?
For UK, ask	Where do you come from?	Are you from (Spain, etc.)?
For non-UK, ask	Where do you live?	Do you live in … (name of district / town etc.)?
	Thank you.	
	A, do you work or are you a student?	Do you work? Do you study? Are you a student?
For UK, ask	Where do you come from?	Are you from (Spain, etc.)?
For non-UK, ask	Where do you live?	Do you live in … (name of district / town etc.)?
	Thank you.	

Phase 2

Interlocutor

Now, let's talk about **holidays**.

Back-up prompts

A, when do you like going on holiday?

Do you like going on holiday in the summer?

How do you usually travel when you go on holiday?

Do you usually travel by car when you go on holiday?

B, who do you go on holiday with?

Do you go on holiday with your family?

Where do you like to eat when you're on holiday?

Do you like to eat at restaurants when you're on holiday?

Extended Response
Now, **A**, please tell me something about your last holiday.

Back-up questions
Where did you go on your last holiday?
What was the weather like?
Did you buy anything special?

Interlocutor

Now, let's talk about **your home**.

Back-up prompts

B, what kind of building do you live in?

Do you live in a flat?

How much time do you spend at home?

Do you spend a lot of time at home?

A, which room do you like best in your home?

Do you like your bedroom best?

What do you enjoy doing at home?

Do you enjoy listening to music at home?

Extended Response
Now, **B**, please tell me something about the different rooms in your home.

Back-up questions
How many rooms are there in your home?
Which is the biggest room in your home?
What is your sitting room like?

Part 2 (5–6 minutes)

Phase 1

Interlocutor
🕐 *3–4 minutes*

Now, in this part of the test you are going to talk together.

*Place **Part 2** booklet, open at **Test 4**, in front of candidates.*

Here are some pictures that show **different sports**.

Do you like these different sports? Say why or why not. I'll say that again.

Do you like these different sports? Say why or why not.

All right? Now, talk together.

Candidates
....

🕐 *Allow a minimum of 1 minute (maximum of 2 minutes) before moving on to the following questions.*

Interlocutor /
Candidates
Use as appropriate.
Ask each candidate
at least one question.

Do you think …
… playing rugby is dangerous?
… swimming is healthy?
… skiing is expensive?
… playing tennis is difficult?
… skateboarding is easy?

Optional prompt
Why? / Why not?
What do **you** think?

Interlocutor

So, **A**, which of these sports do you like best?
And you, **B**, which of these sports do you like best?

Thank you. (Can I have the booklet, please?) *Retrieve **Part 2** booklet.*

Phase 2

Interlocutor
🕐 *Allow up to*
2 minutes

Now, which is more fun, doing sport alone or playing in a team, **B**? (Why?)

And what about you, **A**? (Which is more fun, doing sport alone or playing in a team?) (Why?)

Which do you prefer, watching sport on TV or in a stadium, **A**? (Why?)

And what about you, **B**? (Which do you prefer, watching sport on TV or in a stadium?) (Why?)

Thank you. That is the end of the test.

Test 1 answer key

Reading and Writing

Further feedback available in the downloadable resources

Part 1

1 C   **2** A   **3** C   **4** B   **5** B   **6** B

Part 2

7 B   **8** A   **9** C   **10** A   **11** B   **12** A   **13** B

Part 3

14 B   **15** C   **16** C   **17** B   **18** A

Part 4

19 C   **20** C   **21** B   **22** A   **23** B   **24** A

Part 5

25 up   **26** At   **27** it   **28** for   **29** the   **30** if

Part 6

Sample answer A

> Hello Robbie!
>
> At last weekend I took part in a running competition. At the start I felt pretty nervous I wasn't sure if I can do this. But when I started to run I forgot about everything and felt so relaxed that I won the competition. I was really proud of myself because I have never win anything.
>
> Martyna

Commentary and mark

A very good attempt at the task. The content of the message is relevant to the task and all three elements of the message are clearly communicated, so the reader is fully informed. The text is coherent and connected using basic linking words and cohesive devices (*this, but, the, because*). Everyday vocabulary (*pretty nervous, everything, proud*) is used appropriately and simple grammatical forms are used with a good degree of control (*running, I took part in, At the start I felt, I wasn't sure if, felt so relaxed that*).

Content	5
Organisation	5
Language	5
Total	**15**

Sample answer B

> Dear Robbie
>
> I played football mach on last weekend and I felt very well when I started the mach but when the match finished I was very tired.
>
> Bye and see you soon.

Commentary and mark

A satisfactory attempt at the task. The first two parts of the message have been communicated, but the final part has not been addressed, so the reader is only on the whole informed. The text is connected, using basic linking words (*and, but*). There is some control of grammatical forms (*when I started, I was very tired*), but vocabulary is only basic. Incorrect spelling of *match* is noticeable, but meaning can still be determined.

Content	3
Organisation	3
Language	3
Total	**9**

Part 7

Sample answer A

> One day, Jane was in a market. She bought a bag of fresh fruits. After buying the fruits, Jane walked back to her home.
>
> During the journey, Jane was walking back to her home happily. Suddenly, the bag of fruits broke and all the fruits fell to the ground. Jane was shocked when the fruits fell. She don't know what to do.
>
> Suddenly, Jane thinked of an idea. She took of the hat which she was wearing. After that, she put the fruits into the hat. After putting the fruits into the hat, she continued her journey back home.

Commentary and mark

A very good attempt at the task. All the content points are dealt with and the target reader is fully informed. The text is connected and coherent, using basic linking words and some cohesive devices (*After buying, Suddenly, when, which, After that*). Everyday vocabulary is used appropriately and correctly (*a bag of fresh fruits, the ground, hat, journey*). Simple grammatical forms are used with a good degree of control (*Jane was in, She bought, what to do, which she was wearing*). Errors are minimal (*She don't, took of*).

Content	5
Organisation	5
Language	5
Total	**15**

Sample answer B

> One good morning I go to the market.
>
> I go to one shop next to other shop after to other. Then I have got big packet of food. It was bananas, apples, and many other food. After four shops my packet was broke. I feel very bad. Then I found all food and go to home. It was the worst day of my life.

Commentary and mark

A satisfactory attempt at the task. All parts of the story are communicated. Although the description of picture 2 is not completely clear because of a vocabulary error (*my packet was broke*) meaning can be determined. The text is connected using simple linking words and cohesive devices (*then, and, it*). The story uses basic vocabulary reasonably appropriately (*shop, bananas, apples, worst day*) and simple grammatical forms with some control (*I have got, I found, It was*).

Content	4
Organisation	3
Language	3
Total	**10**

Listening

Part 1

1 C   **2** C   **3** B   **4** B   **5** A

Part 2

6 4.20 / twenty past four / four twenty   **7** blue   **8** 90 / ninety
9 museum   **10** theatre / theater

Part 3

11 A   **12** B   **13** C   **14** C   **15** B

Part 4

16 A   **17** C   **18** A   **19** B   **20** B

Part 5

21 E   **22** G   **23** C   **24** A   **25** F

Further feedback available in the downloadable resources

Transcript

Test One. There are five parts to the test. You will hear each piece twice. We will now stop for a moment before we start the test. Please ask any questions now because you must NOT speak during the test.

PART 1   *Now look at the instructions for Part One.*

For each question, choose the correct answer.

Question 1   *One. How did the woman travel to work this morning?*

Man: Hi, you're late for work today.

Woman: Yes, I couldn't use my car – it's at the garage.

Man: So, did you get the train?

Woman: Well, I was on my way to the station, but got on the wrong bus. It took me to the university instead. I was looking at my phone and didn't notice. Then I had to get another one to get here.

Now listen again.

[repeat]

Question 2   *Two. What will the man eat first at the restaurant?*

Woman: The menu looks really good. What are you going to have?

Man: Well, I want roast chicken for the main course, but I'll have the mushroom soup for my first course.

Woman: I'll have the chicken too, but I'll have salad to start.

Man: I had that last time, but I'm really hungry today. Right, so we're
          ready to order.

Now listen again.

[repeat]

Question 3   *Three. Which was the view from the woman's hotel room?*

Man: Good holiday?

Woman: Fantastic, thanks. The hotel was by the beach. It had a beautiful
          garden. Here's a photo.

Man: Amazing view! I'd love to wake up in a hotel room and see that
          beach.

Woman: Well, my room was on the other side of the hotel, opposite the pool.
          I walked along the beach every day, and around the garden too.

Now listen again.

[repeat]

Question 4   *Four. Why will the man miss the concert tonight?*

Woman: Are you ready to leave soon? The concert starts at 7. Oh no, you
          look really pale. Have you got a bad headache?

Man: There's something wrong with my tooth. It really hurts.

Woman: What about taking some medicine for the pain?

Man: No, thanks, that'll give me a stomach ache.

Woman: OK, well, let me try and get a doctor's appointment for you.

Now listen again.

[repeat]

Question 5   *Five. What will the woman wear for the party?*

Woman: I'm trying to decide what to wear for the party. What do you think of
          this jumper?

Man: It looks great, but won't you be too warm? What about your
          favourite dress?

Woman: I'm not sure. Everyone else will probably be in jeans and T-shirts.

Man: You don't have to wear what everyone else wears!

Woman: Yes, you're right! I'll take your advice!

Now listen again.

[repeat]

That is the end of Part One.

PART 2   *Now look at Part Two.*

*For each question, write the correct answer in the gap. Write one word or a number
or a date or a time. Look at questions 6–10 now. You have ten seconds.*

You will hear a man giving information about a city bus tour.

Man: Welcome to City Bus Tours. My name's Greg. We'll start our tour at ten o'clock. There's another tour at one thirty and a final one at twenty past four. There are lots of people this morning, so it might be better to do a later tour instead. If you decide to do that, you need to know the colour of the bus stop. Wait at the blue one – the green stop's for the normal city buses, not tourist buses.

Some of you've asked how long the tour takes. It's about 90 minutes, and I'll talk for around 40 minutes of that to tell you about the city.

Don't lose your bus ticket, as you can use it to get a discount at one of the most interesting places in the city – that's the museum behind the stadium.

You need to know where the tour finishes. As you can see, we're outside the university now, and the last place we'll see is the theatre. From there you can easily get to the river.

Now listen again.

[repeat]

That is the end of Part Two.

PART 3   *Now look at Part Three.*

For each question, choose the correct answer. Look at questions 11–15 now. You have twenty seconds.

You will hear two friends, Richard and Barbara, talking about a new supermarket.

Richard: Have you been to the new supermarket, Barbara?

Barbara: Yes, Richard, it's great!

Richard: I went this morning. And I couldn't believe it's so large when you get inside!

Barbara: Were there many people?

Richard: Not really. But it was early.

Barbara: And you can save money on your shopping.

Richard: Yeah. Every week, there are special offers on one kind of food, like meat for example. It's fruit at the moment.

Barbara: And next week it might be… vegetables?

Richard: I suppose.

Barbara: So, what did you like best?

Richard: Well, one of the staff told me about the café, but I didn't have enough time to go. People don't usually like the songs they hear in supermarkets, but I loved them there!

Barbara: Me too.

Richard: But I had a problem.

Barbara: You had to wait to pay?

Richard: Not really. I had to pay by cash, but I prefer using my credit card.

Barbara: What a shame.

Richard: Did you use the car park?

Barbara: Yes, I found it easily. You have to walk a long way to get to the supermarket, but at least anybody can park all day.

Now listen again.

[repeat]

That is the end of Part Three.

PART 4   *Now look at Part Four.*

For each question, choose the correct answer.

Question 16   *Sixteen. You will hear a woman talking on the radio about her job. What's her job?*

Woman: I guess I've always enjoyed either building or taking things apart – ever since I was a little girl. As a teenager, I loved nothing more than helping my dad fix vehicles or working in his garage. So, it wasn't a big surprise when I chose a career where I design and build planes. I've had an amazing time so far.

Now listen again.

[repeat]

Question 17   *Seventeen. You will hear a woman talking to a friend about a film. What does she say about the film?*

Man: Have you seen any good films recently?

Woman: Yes, last week. I usually watch comedies, but I wanted to watch something different, so I chose a horror film – I was a bit afraid some of the time!

Man: It still sounds like a good film, but I prefer ones that are based on facts.

Woman: Well, this one certainly wasn't!

Now listen again.

[repeat]

Question 18   *Eighteen. You will hear a sports coach talking to some footballers. What would the coach like them to become better at?*

Man: You did much better in last Saturday's match. Well done for scoring two goals! They were a great team and you almost beat them. What you need to improve is moving fast around the field when you've got the ball. That's what we'll practise today. I'm going to divide you into four small teams and we'll work together to do this.

Now listen again.

[repeat]

Question 19   *Nineteen. You will hear two friends talking about a website. Why does Julia prefer to buy clothes from the website?*

Man: That's a nice sweater, Julia.

Woman: Thanks, it's from HighFashion.com – I always order from there.

Man:	Their men's clothes are all right, if you don't mind wearing stuff that isn't very popular anymore.
Woman:	I don't care about that because everything's at least half-price. But orders can take a while before I get them in the mail.
Man:	Yeah, other sites are faster that way.

Now listen again.

[repeat]

Question 20   *Twenty. You will hear two colleagues talking together. Why was the man not at the meeting this morning?*

Man:	How was the meeting this morning, Charlotte?
Woman:	Good. But why weren't you there? Did you have a dentist's appointment or something?
Man:	That's tomorrow. But one of our most important customers was ill yesterday – he had a terrible earache – so he wanted to see me today. Unfortunately, that meant missing the meeting.
Woman:	OK. Well, let me tell you what we discussed.

Now listen again.

[repeat]

That's the end of Part Four.

PART 5   *Now look at Part Five.*

For each question, choose the correct answer. Look at questions 21–25 now. You have fifteen seconds.

You will hear Gregory talking to Angelika about some things he has bought for his new house. What is he going to put in each place?

Angelika:	Where are you going to put all these things, Gregory?
Gregory:	I like eating in the garden when it's hot, Angelika, so this table's going outside.
Angelika:	I thought it was for your dining room.
Gregory:	I've already got a table in there. I got this little light to go on it.
Angelika:	That'll look good – it's the same colour as the curtains already in there.
Gregory:	That's true.
Angelika:	Did you get something to go in your bathroom, too? This mirror, maybe.
Gregory:	The wooden chair, actually. I think it'll look good next to the bath.
Angelika:	Nice idea. And what about your bedroom?
Gregory:	I thought about putting this bookcase in there. But I think this little cupboard will look nicer than the bookcase.
Angelika:	There's a space in the living room, a perfect place for the bookcase, you know, under the mirror.
Gregory:	That's a good idea.

Angelika: Yes, do you think the kitchen's a good place to put this clock?

Gregory: That's a present for my parents, actually.

Angelika: Oh! But there's lots of light in there, so why don't you put the mirror in there?

Gregory: Good idea!

Now listen again.

[repeat]

That is the end of Part Five.

You now have six minutes to write your answers on the answer sheet.

[ping]

You have one more minute.

[ping]

That is the end of the test.

Test 2 answer key

Reading and Writing

Part 1

1 C   **2** B   **3** A   **4** B   **5** A   **6** A

Part 2

7 B   **8** C   **9** A   **10** C   **11** B   **12** C   **13** A

Part 3

14 A   **15** C   **16** A   **17** C   **18** B

Part 4

19 C   **20** B   **21** B   **22** A   **23** C   **24** A

Part 5

25 Do / Can   **26** to   **27** is   **28** we   **29** When   **30** but / (al)though / however

Part 6
Sample answer A

> Hi Pat
>
> Our picnic starts at 2pm on Saturday.
>
> It is in Regan's park, this park is pretty big so we can meet next to the main gate.
>
> You can bring some snacks and water.
>
> If you want you can bring your dog.
>
> Hugs.
>
> Lilia

Commentary and mark

A very good attempt at the task. The content of the message is relevant to the task and all three parts of the message are clearly communicated. The text is coherent and connected using basic linking words and cohesive devices appropriately (*It, this, so, and*). Simple grammatical forms are used with good control (*starts at, we can meet, You can bring, If you want*). Everyday vocabulary is used appropriately (*pretty big, snacks and water*) and there are no errors.

Content	5
Organisation	5
Language	5
Total	**15**

Sample answer B

> Hello picnic on Saturday well at 5 o'clock.
>
> We meet in park. You need a neptice, blancet, and sousege, bread, water.

Commentary and mark

A satisfactory attempt at the task. All three content points are addressed, so the reader is fully informed. Although the candidate has attempted to use punctuation and a basic linking word (*and*) to help with organisation, the text is not very well connected. The candidate has used some basic relevant vocabulary (*park, bread, water*) and some simple grammatical forms are used with some degree of control (*at 5 o'clock, You need*). Errors may impede meaning (*on Saturday well, neptice, blancet, and sousege*).

Content	5
Organisation	2
Language	2
Total	**9**

Part 7

Sample answer A

> Lucy was very happy because today is her's friend's birthday party. So Lucy went to the street to buy any dress for the party. Then, whlie walking she saw a beautiful dress, so, she bought that dress.
>
> In the evening, she dressed up and wear hear assecories on her dressing table. So, she start her car and drive the car to the house.
>
> When, she arrived there she was shocked because she saw onther women was wearing the same dress. Than the sat down and talk. After that they become friends.

Commentary and mark

A very good attempt at the task. All the content points are dealt with and the target reader is fully informed. The text is coherent and connected, using basic linking words and some cohesive devices (*because, The, her, there*). Everyday vocabulary is used appropriately (*birthday party, beautiful dress, dressing table*). Simple grammatical forms are used correctly (*was very happy, she saw, she dressed up, was wearing*). Errors are noticeable, but meaning can still be determined (*hers friend's, wear hear assecories, she saw onther women*).

Content	5
Organisation	5
Language	5
Total	**15**

Sample answer B

> A girl saw a beautiful clothes. She bought they. at the evening she is going to go to the party. She weared the clothes on the party. Her friend has the same clothes what she had.

Commentary and mark

A satisfactory attempt at the task. The description of the first picture is incomplete and the second picture is only addressed minimally. There is some attempt at organisation using punctuation, but linking is affected by language errors (*she bought they, the same clothes what she had*). There is some appropriate use of basic vocabulary (*party, evening*). Simple grammatical forms are used with some control (*She bought, to go to, she had*).

Content	3
Organisation	2
Language	3
Total	**8**

Listening

↓ Further feedback available in the downloadable resources

Part 1

1 B **2** A **3** A **4** A **5** C

Part 2

6 6.30 / six thirty / half past six / half past 6 **7** Sky
8 swimsuit **9** 18 / eighteen **10** Harcourt

Part 3

11 B **12** A **13** C **14** C **15** A

Part 4

16 B **17** C **18** B **19** B **20** B

Part 5

21 E **22** D **23** G **24** A **25** H

Transcript

Test Two. There are five parts to the test. You will hear each piece twice. We will now stop for a moment before we start the test. Please ask any questions now because you must NOT speak during the test.

PART 1 *Now look at the instructions for Part One.*

For each question, choose the correct answer.

Question 1 *One. Where is the cup now?*

Woman: I can't find my favourite cup anywhere, Joe. Do you know where it is?

Man: Look in the cupboard. That's where it usually is.

Woman: I did. And on the shelf next to the cupboard.

Man: Oh, sorry, I think I left it by the sink when I finished the washing-up.

Woman: Thanks.

Now listen again.

[repeat]

Question 2 *Two. Who will Sally meet at the station?*

Man: My sister's arriving at the station at six. Can you pick her up, Sally?

Woman: Of course. Is it your younger sister – the one with long black hair?

Man: No, the older one – you haven't met her yet.

Woman: I think you showed me her photo. Does she have short hair?

Man: That's her – she's blonde.

Now listen again.

[repeat]

Question 3   *Three. What did the man learn to do at the beach?*

Woman: How was your trip?

Man: It was brilliant. I really enjoyed swimming – the sea was so warm.

Woman: Lucky you!

Man: And I met some great people who showed me how to play volleyball, I've not done it before. And it was great to see surfing. I'd love to learn, and I think I'll have lessons next year.

Now listen again.

[repeat]

Question 4   *Four. Where are they going to meet?*

Man: Do you want to go to the cinema this evening and see that film?

Woman: OK. And we could go and eat something first.

Man: All right. Why don't I wait for you outside the bookshop at about six?

Woman: I'll come and find you there when I finish work. Then we can go and look for a restaurant before the film.

Now listen again.

[repeat]

Question 5   *Five. What didn't the man buy?*

Woman: Did you get everything for our ski trip? Did you find some nice new gloves?

Man: Not the ones I wanted, but these warm ones were on sale. Sunglasses weren't in the sale, but I liked these so much I got them.

Woman: Cool. And did you get a scarf?

Man: I don't think I need a new one. The one I've already got is fine.

Now listen again.

[repeat]

That is the end of Part One.

PART 2   *Now look at Part Two.*

For each question, write the correct answer in the gap. Write one word or a number or a date or a time. Look at questions 6–10 now. You have ten seconds.

You will hear a woman talking to sailing club members about a trip.

Woman: For the next trip, we'll sail round to Southway Point and back. It's on the 19th of July, and we'll leave at 8 in the morning, but please note this trip is longer than usual. We usually arrive back at the club at 5, but this time we'll return at six thirty in the evening.

We'll sail all morning and stop for lunch in Eastley harbour. This year, we'll go to a café called Sky – there are pictures of clouds on the walls, it's lovely!

You should bring a swimsuit because if the weather's good, we'll dive off the boat. We have lots of towels, so there's no need for you to bring one.

I know we took 20 people last time, but this time the boat's smaller, so we can only take 18. The cost of the trip is £10 per person and if you want to go, give your name to Ms Harcourt, our new club secretary. I'll spell her surname – H-A-R-C-O-U-R-T. She's here every morning.

Now listen again.

[repeat]

That is the end of Part Two.

PART 3   *Now look at Part Three.*

For each question, choose the correct answer. Look at questions 11–15 now. You have twenty seconds.

You will hear a manager, Victoria, talking to her assistant, Daniel, about the new company building.

Daniel: Victoria, how shall we tell staff about the new company building?

Victoria: I'll tell everyone at the same time, Daniel. We can use our largest office. And, by the way, I'd like the staff barbeque to be a surprise. I'll email everyone the details later.

Daniel: Shall we tell them why we're moving to a new building?

Victoria: Yes, I'll explain that because we'll be ten kilometres away from the centre, the rent's much lower, but that the offices are the same size.

Daniel: Sure. Today's May 31st, so when will we be in the new building?

Victoria: Let's say by July 1st staff must start packing. Then August 15th will be the first day in their new offices.

Daniel: OK.

Victoria: Perhaps staff will want to know what's near the building.

Daniel: Like the great sports centre across the road – but the cafés around there don't look very nice and the shopping centre looks small.

Victoria: Yes.

Daniel: You've asked me to order a few things. I've bought the signs that we'll need. And I must remember to get keys for everyone. We're using the same desks and chairs.

Victoria: Good.

Now listen again.

[repeat]

That is the end of Part Three.

PART 4   *Now look at Part Four.*

For each question, choose the correct answer.

Question 16   *Sixteen. You will hear a woman, Jen, telling her friend about her favourite singer, Mikey. What's just happened?*

Woman: I've just seen Mikey – my favourite singer!

Man: Wow, Jen, you've been to his concert?

Woman: The tickets were too expensive for me, unfortunately, so I waited outside the theatre.

Man: Did you get a chance to speak to him?

Woman: He waved and I got a picture, but that's all. I shouted *hello*, but he didn't hear me. He was in a hurry.

Now listen again.

[repeat]

Question 17   *Seventeen. You will hear a man, Alex, talking to a friend about a tennis competition. Why didn't Alex do well in the competition?*

Woman: Hi Alex, how was the tennis competition?

Man: I didn't play very well – I went to bed really late the night before.

Woman: It's horrible playing when you don't have enough energy. I remember once I didn't eat all day and then I played a match.

Man: I know it's really important to have plenty to eat and drink before a competition.

Now listen again.

[repeat]

Question 18   *Eighteen. You will hear two people talking at a tourist information centre. What advice does the man give the woman?*

Woman: What can you tell me about the National Museum? I'd like to go there this afternoon.

Man: Well, there's always so much going on at the museum. The exhibitions are all worth visiting. But don't spend money on tickets now.

Woman: Why's that?

Man: Tomorrow's the only day in August when you won't have to pay. And that offer even includes the special exhibitions.

Now listen again.

[repeat]

Question 19   *Nineteen. You will hear two friends talking about what they did at the weekend. What didn't the woman do at the weekend?*

Man: Did you play basketball this weekend, Katy?

Woman: I couldn't. I'd hurt my leg. But I watched an amazing game on TV on Sunday afternoon.

Man:	I saw that too. So, were you at home all weekend?
Woman:	No. I had a great time in town with a friend on Saturday morning. I got myself some great new trainers. They're really smart.

Now listen again.

[repeat]

Question 20 *Twenty. You will hear a man talking to his friend about his new flat. What's he going to do now?*

Man:	Thanks for helping me move in, the apartment's looking great. I'm glad we decided to put the bookcase in the corner. It didn't look right next to the door. I'm not sure about the colour of the walls, but I can change that later. It's really cold in here though, so I've got to do something about that immediately.

Now listen again.

[repeat]

That is the end of Part Four.

PART 5 *Now look at Part Five.*

For each question, choose the correct answer. Look at questions 21–25 now. You have fifteen seconds.

You will hear a woman telling her brother about her friends and their hobbies. What hobby does each friend have?

Woman:	I was thinking, most of my friends just have one hobby.
Man:	Right. Like Simon?
Woman:	Yes. He's always drawing and painting.
Man:	I know. And what does Jane like doing?
Woman:	Taking pictures. Especially black and white.
Man:	Oh yes, I saw one she took of a guy reading a book. It was brilliant.
Woman:	She's really good.
Man:	Yeah.
Woman:	And Derek. He's in a rock band. Actually, they're playing at the theatre next week.
Man:	Oh, we should go!
Woman:	Sure. And you know Mary?
Man:	I think so.
Woman:	Well, she's been to so many countries. But she never takes any photos – she says she's too busy.
Man:	Right! And isn't Tony a big football fan?
Woman:	Not these days. But he's been in some plays this year. He's good on stage! He was in one about a musician.

Man: Oh yes, I read about that online.

Woman: And Sarah, well, she goes to see the local basketball matches most
           weekends. And recently, she paid 80 dollars just to see a cycle race!

Now listen again.

[repeat]

That is the end of Part Five.

You now have six minutes to write your answers on the answer sheet.

[ping]

You have one more minute.

[ping]

That is the end of the test.

Test 3 answer key

Reading and Writing

Further feedback available in the downloadable resources

Part 1

1 A   **2** B   **3** C   **4** A   **5** A   **6** C

Part 2

7 B   **8** C   **9** B   **10** A   **11** C   **12** A   **13** B

Part 3

14 A   **15** C   **16** B   **17** A   **18** B

Part 4

19 C   **20** C   **21** A   **22** C   **23** A   **24** B

Part 5

25 next / this   **26** what   **27** any / some   **28** as   **29** by   **30** your

Part 6

Sample answer A

> Hi, Alex!
>
> Let's meet near the supermarket and go to the square together. I'll be waiting for you at 2 p.m. I can bring a few sandwiches, so may you bring a bottle of water, please?

Commentary and mark

A very good attempt at the task. All the content points are addressed, so the target reader is fully informed. The text is coherent and connected using basic linking words effectively (*and, so*). Vocabulary is used appropriately and correctly. Simple grammatical forms (*Let's meet, I'll be waiting, I can bring*) and everyday vocabulary (*the supermarket, a few sandwiches, a bottle of water*) are used appropriately and with good control.

Content	5
Organisation	5
Language	5
Total	**15**

Sample answer B

> Good morning, Alex!
>
> We meet near the "Hotel Eleon", or near the cafe "Sky". Coues where we meet. Came there in 8:15am. Don't late, please. Good byae

Commentary and mark

A satisfactory attempt at the task. The candidate has not told Alex what to bring, but the other content points are addressed. The text is connected using some basic linking words and cohesive devices (*or, where, there*). The message uses simple grammatical forms with some control (*near the cafe, We can go*), but some errors (*Coues where we meet*) impede communication.

Content	3
Organisation	3
Language	2
Total	**8**

Part 7
Sample answer A

> ### An Exciting Day
>
> I was watching the television one day during the holidays. It was an exciting news. The news was about a tsunami. At that time, I was so scared and terrified.
>
> Suddenly, there was a power failure happened in my house. "Oh dear! What shall I do?" I decided to phone my friend. It was hot when it has a power failure.
>
> I decided to go to my friend's house to invite her to a movie in the nearby cinema. We went to the cinema happily. "Wow! It was a fantastic movie!" I am so glad that I get to see that movie with my friend during the holidays!

Commentary and mark

A very good attempt at the task. All of the content of the story is relevant to the task and the story is connected and coherent using basic linking words and cohesive devices (*It was, Suddenly, her, that*), so the reader can fully understand the story. Everyday vocabulary is generally used appropriately (*power failure, movie, cinema*). The candidate uses simple grammatical forms with a good degree of control (*I was watching, What shall I do?, I decided to go*). Errors are minimal.

Content	5
Organisation	5
Language	5
Total	**15**

Sample answer B

> Sally watch TV at 10:00 p.m. It's would traeler at the film. Sally order the ticket for the film. She goes to the cinema. She sit and watch film, she very funny.

Commentary and mark

A satisfactory attempt at task. The three parts of the story are communicated, but errors may impede meaning at times (*It's would traeler*) so that the reader is not quite fully informed. The text is minimally connected using the basic linking word (*and*). The candidate has used some basic relevant vocabulary (*TV, ticket, cinema, film*), and some simple grammatical forms are used with some degree of control (*order the ticket, She goes*).

Content	4
Organisation	2
Language	3
Total	**9**

Listening

Part 1

1 A   **2** C   **3** B   **4** B   **5** B

Part 2

6 doctor   **7** Caratopia   **8** 24 July
9 8.15 / eight fifteen   **10** 10.50

Part 3

11 A   **12** B   **13** A   **14** C   **15** B

Part 4

16 B   **17** B   **18** B   **19** A   **20** C

Part 5

21 B   **22** D   **23** F   **24** H   **25** C

Further feedback available in the downloadable resources

Transcript

Test Three. There are five parts to the test. You will hear each piece twice. We will now stop for a moment before we start the test. Please ask any questions now because you must NOT speak during the test.

PART 1   *Now look at the instructions for Part One.*

For each question, choose the correct answer.

Question 1   *One. Where will they go if it rains tomorrow?*

Man: My weather app says it might rain tomorrow.

Woman: Oh… we won't be able to go walking. Shall we go out for lunch instead?

Man: I need some exercise. I've been at my desk all week.

Woman: So let's go for a game of badminton. I know you prefer swimming, but the pool will be too busy.

Man: I'll get the rackets.

Now listen again.

[repeat]

Question 2   *Two. Why didn't the woman buy the book?*

Woman: I didn't get the book that you want today. Sorry!

Man: Oh! Was the shop really crowded, as usual?

Woman: Actually, it looked OK, but when I was outside, I met my friend Sophie. We decided to go for a coffee.

Man: And was the shop closed when you finished?

Woman: Well, it was still open, but I'll have more time tomorrow.

Now listen again.

[repeat]

Question 3   *Three. Where does the man work now?*

Woman: I haven't seen you at the supermarket for a while, Bryan.

Man: I left last month, actually. I was only working there until I finished my mechanics course.

Woman: So, you're finally doing what you've always wanted to do.

Man: I am. I'm working at that place next to the Italian restaurant.

Woman: I'll bring my car there next time I have a problem.

Now listen again.

[repeat]

Question 4   *Four. Where does the man want to go?*

Woman: Do you need some help?

Man: Yes! Thank you. I'm looking for the museum. On my map it looks quite near to the castle, but we're outside the castle now, and I can't see it.

Woman: Well, it's not far. Walk down this hill, and it's on your right. There's a nice café opposite.

Man: That's great. Thank you again.

Now listen again.

[repeat]

Question 5   *Five. What's the man making?*

Woman: Mmm... lovely! Are you making a fruit cake?

Man: I'm adding the dried fruit to the bread that I'm baking. We can have it with cheese tonight, and use the rest for toast tomorrow morning. If you want cake, there's a slice left in the fridge.

Woman: That's OK. I'll wait for supper. Shall I make a fruit salad for dessert?

Man: Yes, please.

Now listen again.

[repeat]

That is the end of Part One.

PART 2   *Now look at Part Two.*

For each question, write the correct answer in the gap. Write one word or a number or a date or a time. Look at questions 6–10 now. You have ten seconds.

You will hear a man talking about a film on local radio.

Man:	You'll be able to see a very special film in the city this weekend. It's called *Runner*, and it was actually filmed in our own city – it's a really exciting story. This new film's about a doctor and the star is John Hughes, who was very successful in his last film, called *Stage*, which was about a rock band. They're showing it at the Caratopia Cinema – that's spelled C-A-R-A-T-O-P-I-A, which is a small cinema near the town square.

You can see it from the 24th to the 31st of July. Also, on the 28th of July some of the actors will come to talk about the film and answer your questions. Anyway, the film begins at quarter past eight and is an hour and a half long, so it'll finish at quarter to ten.

It's a good idea to book tickets. If you're studying, they're ten pounds fifty, and they're thirteen pounds thirty for everyone else. You can find more information about this interesting film on our website.

Now listen again.

[repeat]

That is the end of Part Two.

PART 3   *Now look at Part Three.*

For each question, choose the correct answer. Look at questions 11–15 now. You have twenty seconds.

You will hear Phil talking to his friend Jess about a new sports centre.

Phil:	Hi, Jess. Did you hear about the new sports centre on the radio this morning?
Jess:	The one that you and your friend Bob went to? No... actually, there was a poster about it near my work. Is it good?
Phil:	Yes, it's bigger than the old one and it's fun, especially with the great loud music they play! It costs a lot. Too much.
Jess:	Do you go every day?
Phil:	If I can. Mornings are best because it's less busy, especially very early. Schools use it during the day, but that's fine because I'm at work then. Weekends are too crowded.
Jess:	The pool in the old sports centre's quite dirty, so I'd love to try this new one. I'd like to enter one of their swimming competitions, but the heating for the water isn't working, so it's not open yet.
Phil:	Let's go to the gym together instead!
Jess:	I'm not a member and I need new trainers.
Phil:	That doesn't matter. You can join when you get there, and we'll go to the café afterwards – it's cheaper for members. So are the classes.
Jess:	OK, great.

Now listen again.

[repeat]

That is the end of Part Three.

PART 4   *Now look at Part Four.*

For each question, choose the correct answer.

Question 16   *Sixteen. You will hear a woman talking to a friend about getting to work. Why did the woman arrive at the office late?*

Man: You're never late for work! What happened? Did you lose your keys or something?

Woman: My keys weren't the problem.

Man: Was it because of the road repairs?

Woman: The road that I usually take was fine, it wasn't busy. My engine stopped and I couldn't start it again. Luckily, I didn't have to wait long at the side of the road for help.

Now listen again.

[repeat]

Question 17   *Seventeen. You will hear a man, Peter, talking to a friend about his plans. Where will Peter be this Saturday?*

Woman: Hi Peter, there's a sailing course I'd like to do at Blue Water Lake on Saturday. Would you like to come?

Man: I'd love to, but I'm going on a foreign business trip… Oh! I've still got to change some money.

Woman: Oh, what about the following weekend?

Man: I'm really sorry, it's my mum's birthday and we've planned a celebration.

Woman: Never mind!

Now listen again.

[repeat]

Question 18   *Eighteen. You will hear a man talking about a music festival. What's different about the festival this year?*

Man: Don't miss this year's rock music festival! It's more and more popular every year! That's why all the stages are in the park, because the town square can no longer handle the crowds for this exciting festival. It's the summer festival, so put it in your calendar. And it's always the last weekend in August. Tickets are on sale now.

Now listen again.

[repeat]

Question 19   *Nineteen. You will hear two people talking about their school days. Which subject did they both enjoy at school?*

Man: Was science your favourite lesson when we were at school?

Woman: Well, I loved those chemistry experiments we did.

Man: Oh? I didn't. I thought learning about life in Rome centuries ago was much more interesting.

| Woman: | I agree. All those amazing buildings they created. I thought the most boring lessons at school were when we had to draw maps of different countries. |
| Man: | You're right! |

Now listen again.

[repeat]

Question 20 *Twenty. You will hear someone talking to customers in a supermarket. What's cheaper in the supermarket this week?*

| Woman: | Welcome to your local supermarket. This week we have fantastic new chocolate ice cream – it's only four pounds ninety-nine for one litre! Grapes and pears are half price. If you're planning a party, we now sell extra large bottles of lemonade. If you need help finding things, please ask. |

Now listen again.

[repeat]

That is the end of Part Four.

PART 5 *Now look at Part Five.*

For each question, choose the correct answer. Look at questions 21–25 now. You have fifteen seconds.

You will hear Helena talking to her friend Steve about hotels in their city. What does Steve think about each hotel?

Helena:	Steve?
Steve:	Yes, Helena.
Helena:	I need to book a hotel in the city for some Australian friends of mine. I've heard Plaza Hotel's good. Do you know it?
Steve:	My sister stayed there. She drove around for an hour looking for it. There are no signs to show you where it is.
Helena:	What about City Hotel?
Steve:	Beautiful old building, especially the dining room. Your friends would love it. Of course, it's not cheap.
Helena:	That's no good.
Steve:	There's the Bridge Hotel. They often have special prices. There's a fantastic chef there – he's won competitions.
Helena:	Sounds nice. Do you know Lemontree Hotel?
Steve:	I've looked at their website. Their bedrooms are much bigger than in most other hotels. It's on a quiet street with lots of parking places.
Helena:	Right. How about Greenleaf Hotel?
Steve:	It's quite cheap. You hear the traffic when people are going to and from work.
Helena:	And is the International Hotel OK?

Steve: I haven't seen the bedrooms, but the receptionists are very nice. My colleague at work said they're always happy to help.

Helena: OK, thanks... [fade]

Now listen again.

[repeat]

That is the end of Part Five.

You now have six minutes to write your answers on the answer sheet.

[ping]

You have one more minute.

[ping]

That is the end of the test.

Test 4 answer key

Reading and Writing

⬇ Further feedback available in the downloadable resources

Part 1

1 B   **2** C   **3** B   **4** B   **5** A   **6** C

Part 2

7 B   **8** C   **9** A   **10** C   **11** A   **12** B   **13** C

Part 3

14 B   **15** C   **16** C   **17** A   **18** A

Part 4

19 B   **20** A   **21** B   **22** C   **23** C   **24** C

Part 5

25 go / enjoy   **26** a / this   **27** Have   **28** Do   **29** next / this / that   **30** let

Part 6

Sample answer A

> Hi Alex,
>
> Would you like to go to the shopping centre with me on Satuday? I need to buy new shoes because I scratched my last one. We will go to the shopping centre by bus.
>
> Write back soon,
>
> Bozhidara.

Commentary and mark

A very good attempt at the task. All three elements of the message are fully communicated, so the target reader would be fully informed. The text is connected and coherent, but *because* is the only cohesive device used accurately. Grammatical forms are well controlled (*Would you like to, We will go, by bus*). Vocabulary is used reasonably appropriately, but there is too much repetition of language from the task (*to the shopping centre, on Satuday, I need to buy*).

Content	5
Organisation	4
Language	4
Total	**13**

Sample answer B

> Hi, Alex.
>
> Well I want to go to the shopping and I ask you If you can go on Saturday to the shopping centre.
>
> In first place I want to buy clothes and I hear, you so good to pick up clothes. And I want to go there because the clothes are less expensive.
>
> If you can do it, can you translade me in your car? because I don't like walk so much.
>
> thanks.
>
> Justin

Commentary and mark

A satisfactory attempt at the task. All three content points are addressed. The text is connected, using a range of linking words and some cohesive devices (*and, there, because*). There is some control of grammatical forms (*If you can go on Saturday, the clothes are less expensive*). It uses basic vocabulary (*clothes, car*), but the errors (*I hear, you so good to pick up clothes, can you translade me*) may impede communication.

Content	5
Organisation	3
Language	3
Total	**11**

Part 7
Sample answer A

> Two friends Nastiya and Jura traveled to bay by ship. They liked nature and animals, so they decited to travel to the jungle to saw monkey. It was hot sunny day, and they wore T-shirts. Their travel was very long, and by the end of travel Nastiya and Jura were very tired. They stoped to have some rest, but suddanly, Nastiya heard noises. Between the trees were lots of monkeies. They climed on the trees and shauted. Nastiya and Jura took a lot of photos. When they went to home, they were very happy.

Commentary and mark

A good attempt at task. All three content points of the story are communicated and, although the first picture is only described briefly, the target reader is fully informed. The text is coherent and uses   some basic linking words and cohesive devices (*and, so, they, their, when*). Basic vocabulary is used reasonably appropriately. The candidate uses simple grammatical forms with some degree of control (*they liked, they wore, were very tired*). Errors are noticeable, especially with spelling, but meaning can still be determined (*traveled to bay, to saw monkey, suddanly, shauted*).

Content	4
Organisation	4
Language	4
Total	**12**

Sample answer B

> Once upon a time, there is two persons; a man and a woman on the beach, it was a afternoon. They come down near the beach and begin to walk in the place where there is the green flowers and have taken the pictures of animals.

Commentary and mark

A satisfactory attempt at task. Although the first picture is not mentioned in the text, the rest of the story is mainly communicated clearly. The reader is on the whole informed. The text is connected using basic linking words and a limted number of cohesive devices (*and, where*). The candidate has used some basic relevant vocabulary (*on the beach, flowers, pictures of animals*), and some simple grammatical forms are used with some degree of control (*it was, have taken*).

Content	3
Organisation	3
Language	3
Total	**9**

Listening

Part 1

1 B   **2** C   **3** C   **4** A   **5** A

Part 2

6 Wednesday   **7** 6.15 / six fifteen   **8** E29 / E-29
9 Halliday   **10** December

Part 3

11 B   **12** A   **13** B   **14** A   **15** B

Part 4

16 C   **17** B   **18** A   **19** C   **20** A

Part 5

21 F   **22** H   **23** C   **24** D   **25** B

Transcript

Test Four. There are five parts to the test. You will hear each piece twice. We will now stop for a moment before we start the test. Please ask any questions now because you must NOT speak during the test.

PART 1   *Now look at the instructions for Part One.*

For each question, choose the correct answer.

Question 1   *One. What was the weather like for the football match?*

Woman: Hi, Harry. How are you? Is it still raining?

Man: Yes. It's a good thing it wasn't like this for the football yesterday.

Woman: Was it sunny for the match?

Man: Well, actually it was quite cloudy, but at least it wasn't wet.

Woman: That's the important thing.

Now listen again.

[repeat]

Question 2   *Two. What sport is the woman going to start doing soon?*

Woman: Hi, how are you? Are you on your way to play football?

Man: I am. You're still doing lots to keep fit I see.

Woman: Yes, but I'm a bit bored of running. Actually, I'm on my way to buy a bike now, so you'll see me out on that next time.

Man: Well, it's always good to try something new!

Now listen again.

[repeat]

Question 3   *Three. Why was the man late for work?*

Woman: Alex, you're late! Is everything OK?

Man: I got up as soon as I heard the alarm clock, and I was at the bus stop five minutes before the bus arrived. But there was so much traffic that it took longer than normal to get here. Sorry!

Woman: Well, tomorrow you should wake up earlier and get an earlier bus!

Man: You're right.

Now listen again.

[repeat]

Question 4   *Four. Which food is the man eating?*

Woman: Mmm, that looks lovely. Was it easy to make?

Man: Yes, you cook the onions and the meat together in a pan, then put in the tomatoes. It's just as easy as making a pizza.

Woman: How long do you have to cook the pasta for?

Man: About ten minutes. It's quicker to make a sandwich, but it doesn't taste as good.

Now listen again.

[repeat]

Question 5   *Five. What has the man had problems with?*

Woman: Can I help you?

Man: Yes, I bought some things here last week. The gloves kept my hands really warm, but look what's happened to these.

Woman: Oh dear!

Man: I only went walking in the mountains in them once. I wore a good pair of socks with them too.

Woman: But these aren't strong enough for doing that. They're for wearing in town.

Now listen again.

[repeat]

That is the end of Part One.

PART 2   *Now look at Part Two.*

For each question, write the correct answer in the gap. Write one word or a number or a date or a time. Look at questions 6–10 now. You have ten seconds.

You will hear some information about music classes at a local college.

Man: Hi, this is a message for Kiera. You wanted some information about a music class. The class that you're interested in, the guitar class, is just after the piano class that your sister is starting soon.

It's at the same place – the local college – and it's every Wednesday evening. It says Thursday on our website, but this is wrong – this information is from last year and we haven't changed it yet.

You'll need to be there at six fifteen and it ends at seven o'clock. There's a class for advanced students in room D-thirty-four, so don't go in there. The beginners' class, which is the one you need, is in E-twenty-nine.

Your classes will be with a very good teacher called Mrs Halliday, that's spelled H-A-double L-I-D-A-Y.

Oh, and as well as doing the classes, our students can also take part in a concert. There's one for classical music in October, but yours, the rock concert, will be in December. Ring me if you need any other information.

Now listen again.

[repeat]

That is the end of Part Two.

PART 3	*Now look at Part Three.*

For each question, choose the correct answer. Look at questions 11–15 now. You have twenty seconds.

You will hear a man, Ben, and a woman, Emma, talking about Ben's new flat.

Woman:	Hi, Ben. You went to live in your new flat two months ago, didn't you?
Man:	Actually, I've only been there for two weeks, and finished painting it two days ago.
Woman:	Is it very different from your old place?
Man:	Well, it isn't bigger and it isn't on the top floor, so the views aren't as good. But I love that it only takes five minutes to walk to work.
Woman:	Fantastic. And the rooms?
Man:	There's a great shower. And lots of wardrobes in my bedroom, which I like. But my favourite room's where I read, watch TV or talk to friends.
Woman:	Have you got everything you need for your new flat?
Man:	I think so!
Woman:	It's lucky the people who lived there before left their carpets. Did you find somewhere to put those shelves I gave you? They'll look good with the curtains from your mum!
Man:	They will, thanks!
Woman:	I know someone who lives in the same building. He writes articles for newspapers.
Man:	Oh, yes. He lives next door. There's a policeman above me. And I've also met someone from another building who repairs cars.

Now listen again.

[repeat]

That is the end of Part Three.

PART 4   *Now look at Part Four.*

For each question, choose the correct answer.

Question 16   *Sixteen. You will hear a man asking for help with his computer. What's the problem with it?*

Man: Claire, can you look at my PC for me? It seems to be working – I can click on websites and type documents and messages, but it's really difficult to read what I've written on the screen. It's too dark. I've tried turning if off and then turning it on again, but the problem's still there.

Now listen again.

[repeat]

Question 17   *Seventeen. You will hear a woman talking to her husband. Where are they planning to meet the woman's brother?*

Woman: My brother's arriving from California tonight.

Man: Great. Are we going to pick him up or will he come to our flat by train?

Woman: He lands at ten and the trains aren't very frequent in the evenings. So let's go and get him.

Man: OK. We should leave home as soon as we get back from work. We mustn't be late for his flight.

Now listen again.

[repeat]

Question 18   *Eighteen. You will hear an explorer talking on the radio. What was the last place that he visited?*

Man: I love going to the most extreme places in the world, like the Sahara Desert. It's a long time since I crossed it on foot – it was harder than climbing Mount Everest, which I did not long ago. But the most fun was living in the jungle on an island – that was the first trip I made.

Now listen again.

[repeat]

Question 19   *Nineteen. You will hear a man talking to his sister about his new phone. Why did he choose this phone?*

Man: Do you like my new phone?

Woman: What's wrong with the one you've already got?

Man: It's really slow at taking pictures. And the ones I do take aren't clear enough.

| Woman: | But your new phone doesn't look as good as your other one. Would you mind giving me your old phone? Mine's really heavy! |
| Man: | Yes, sure! |

Now listen again.

[repeat]

Question 20   *Twenty. You will hear two colleagues talking about a meeting. How do they feel after the meeting?*

Man:	I'm glad we discussed our new work schedule at the meeting.
Woman:	Me too. I was worried they might offer us fewer hours, so we'd get less money.
Man:	Yeah, work's always really quiet this time of year. Well, almost always. I mean, our hours are actually going up, so we'll earn more.
Woman:	I can't remember the last time that happened.

Now listen again.

[repeat]

That is the end of Part Four.

PART 5   *Now look at Part Five.*

For each question, choose the correct answer. Look at questions 21–25 now. You have fifteen seconds.

You will hear Larry talking to Cara about a friend's birthday. What present will each person give?

Larry:	It's Sandy's birthday party next week, Cara. Have you got her a present?
Cara:	Yes. I've been talking to some of the other people to make sure we don't choose the same thing. I decided to get her some paints and brushes.
Larry:	Great idea. I think Anthea's giving her a bracelet, which she made herself.
Cara:	Lovely – Anthea's very artistic. And what about you, Larry?
Larry:	Well, I know Sandy loves going to concerts, so I'm getting her a photo of that band she likes: you know the one – Soloko.
Cara:	She'll love that. Kerry had almost the same idea – she's buying the story that the lead singer wrote about how he became a musician.
Larry:	How about Tony – what's he getting her?
Cara:	He said he wanted to get her some perfume, but he doesn't have much money, so he decided to get her something sweet to eat.
Larry:	Is Hannah going to the party?
Cara:	Of course – she's Sandy's best friend! She's got her a beautiful leather handbag and showed me a picture of it. It looks really expensive.

Now listen again.

[repeat]

That is the end of Part Five.

You now have six minutes to write your answers on the answer sheet.

[ping]

You have one more minute.

[ping]

That is the end of the test.

Sample answer sheet: Reading and Writing

Cambridge Assessment
English

Candidate Name		Candidate Number	
Centre Name		Centre Number	
Examination Title		Examination Details	
Candidate Signature		Assessment Date	

Supervisor: If the candidate is ABSENT or has WITHDRAWN shade here ○

Key Reading and Writing Candidate Answer Sheet

Instructions
Use a PENCIL (B or HB).
Rub out any answer you want to change with an eraser.

For Parts 1, 2, 3 and 4:
Mark ONE letter for each answer.
For example: If you think A is the right answer to the question, mark your answer sheet like this: **0** [A● B○ C○]

For Part 5:
Write your answers clearly in the spaces next to the numbers (25 to 30) like this:

0 | E N G L I S H |

Write your answers in CAPITAL LETTERS.

Part 1	Part 2	Part 3	Part 4
1 A B C	7 A B C	14 A B C	19 A B C
2 A B C	8 A B C	15 A B C	20 A B C
3 A B C	9 A B C	16 A B C	21 A B C
4 A B C	10 A B C	17 A B C	22 A B C
5 A B C	11 A B C	18 A B C	23 A B C
6 A B C	12 A B C		24 A B C
	13 A B C		

Part 5		Do not write below here			Do not write below here
25		25 1 0 ○ ○	28		28 1 0 ○ ○
26		26 1 0 ○ ○	29		29 1 0 ○ ○
27		27 1 0 ○ ○	30		30 1 0 ○ ○

Put your answers to Writing Parts 6 and 7 on the separate Answer Sheet

Draft

Cambridge Assessment
English

Candidate Name

Candidate Number

Centre Name

Centre Number

Examination Title

Examination Details

Candidate Signature

Assessment Date

Supervisor: If the candidate is ABSENT or has WITHDRAWN shade here ○

Key Writing

Candidate Answer Sheet for Parts 6 and 7

INSTRUCTIONS TO CANDIDATES

Make sure that your name and candidate number are on this sheet.

Write your answers to Writing Parts 6 and 7 on the other side of this sheet.

Use a pencil.

You **must** write within the grey lines.

Do **not** write on the bar codes.

Draft

Sample answer sheet: Reading and Writing

Part 6: Write your answer below.

Part 7: Write your answer below.

Examiner's Use Only

Part 6	C	O	L

Part 7	C	O	L

Draft

© UCLES 2019   Photocopiable

Draft

OFFICE USE ONLY - DO NOT WRITE OR MAKE ANY MARK ABOVE THIS LINE   Page 1 of 1

Cambridge Assessment
English

Candidate Name	
Candidate Number	
Centre Name	
Centre Number	
Examination Title	
Examination Details	
Candidate Signature	
Assessment Date	

Supervisor: If the candidate is ABSENT or has WITHDRAWN shade here ○

Key Listening Candidate Answer Sheet

Instructions
Use a PENCIL (B or HB).
Rub out any answer you want to change with an eraser.

For Parts 1, 3, 4 and 5:
Mark ONE letter for each answer.
For example: If you think A is the right answer to
the question, mark your answer sheet like this:

For Part 2:
Write your answers clearly in the spaces next
to the numbers (6 to 10) like this:

0 ENGLISH

Write your answers in CAPITAL LETTERS.

Part 1

	A	B	C
1	○	○	○
2	○	○	○
3	○	○	○
4	○	○	○
5	○	○	○

Part 2

		Do not write below here
6		6 1 0 ○ ○
7		7 1 0 ○ ○
8		8 1 0 ○ ○
9		9 1 0 ○ ○
10		10 1 0 ○ ○

Part 3

	A	B	C
11	○	○	○
12	○	○	○
13	○	○	○
14	○	○	○
15	○	○	○

Part 4

	A	B	C
16	○	○	○
17	○	○	○
18	○	○	○
19	○	○	○
20	○	○	○

Part 5

	A	B	C	D	E	F	G	H
21	○	○	○	○	○	○	○	○
22	○	○	○	○	○	○	○	○
23	○	○	○	○	○	○	○	○
24	○	○	○	○	○	○	○	○
25	○	○	○	○	○	○	○	○

OFFICE USE ONLY - DO NOT WRITE OR MAKE ANY MARK BELOW THIS LINE   Page 1 of 1

Draft

Acknowledgements

The authors and publishers acknowledge the following sources of copyright material and are grateful for the permissions granted. While every effort has been made, it has not always been possible to identify the sources of all the material used, or to trace all copyright holders. If any omissions are brought to our notice, we will be happy to include the appropriate acknowledgements on reprinting and in the next update to the digital edition, as applicable.

Photographs

Key: T = Test, RW = Reading & Writing, P = Part.

All the photographs are sourced from Getty Images.

T2 RW P2: XiFotos/iStock/Getty Images Plus; Dougal Waters/DigitalVision; SolStock/E+;
T3 RW P2: Javier Sánchez Mingorance/EyeEm; Terry Vine/Blend Images; Bradley Olson/EyeEm;
T4 RW P2: Jose Luis Pelaez Inc/DigitalVision; MaFelipe/E+; Hero Images.

Typeset by QBS Learning.

Audio production by Real Deal Productions and dsound recording Ltd.

Visual materials for the Speaking test

Test 1

Do you like these different types of food?

Test 2
Do you like these different ways of travelling?

Test 3
Do you like these different free-time activities?

Test 4

Do you like these different sports?